SITE AND SURVEY DOWSING

SITE AND SURVEY DOWSING

An anthology from the Journal of the British Society of Dowsers

Edited by Clive Thompson

TURNSTONE PRESS LIMITED
Wellingborough, Northamptonshire

This anthology first published 1980

© jointly British Society of Dowsers and contributory authors 1980

ISBN 0 85500 120 8 (hardback)
    0 85500 121 6 (paperback)

Prepared by Wordsmith Graphics, Street.
Printed and bound in Great Britain by
Weatherby Woolnough, Wellingborough,
Northamptonshire.

Contents

Series Editor's Note

This is the second of a series of anthologies derived from the *Journal of the British Society of Dowsers,* presenting a number of themes in dowsing to a wider audience. The first in the series was on *Dowsing and Archaeology.*

These books are prepared by direct photographic reproduction from the *Journal,* and the print quality of the original does vary in places, as can be expected in a Journal whose issues span nearly fifty years and several changes of printer and printing process. We feel, however, that this is more than compensated for by the quality of the articles!

The opinions presented in the articles in this anthology are not necessarily held by the British Society of Dowsers, or currently even by their authors, as their opinions may have changed with later developments and the passing of time. Some articles have been included more for their historical importance or interest than for their relevance to current dowsing theory or practice.

The British Society of Dowsers was founded in 1933 as a reference point for people interested in all forms of dowsing, whether practical or theoretical. The current Secretary is Mr. Michael Rust, of Court Lodge Farm, Hastingleigh, Ashford, Kent, from whom details of the *Journal* and membership of the Society may be obtained.

Tom Graves

Editor's Introduction

In presenting this collection of articles from the *Journal of the British Society of Dowsers*, my aim is to draw the attention of the reader to the fact that dowsing has evolved, through experience and research, into a very useful site survey aid. Dowsing is used not only for finding water and minerals, but it is now enabling the surveyor, civil engineer, architect and contractor to find all manner of hidden objects and conditions, on sites or within buildings, which are not normally detectable. Examples discussed in this anthology include pipes, cables, conduits, culverts, tunnels, sealed basements, cisterns, old foundations, capped or filled wells, mine and ventilation shafts, underground workings, drains, sewers, broken pipes, hidden man-holes, gas mains, electrical and telephone services, natural cavities, aquifers and other geological conditions. Most site problems are not far below ground or floor surface or deep in wall structures, and may be found simply using dowsing techniques. The finding of aquifers (water-bearing fissures or flows) on building sites is more important than many people realise, for if located prior to the digging of foundations or basements the aquifer can be diverted and flooding prevented. As a method of answering site problems dowsing can provide a great saving in time and expense; particularly so when searches have to be made quickly and under difficult conditions that would otherwise call for costly specialist equipment. The dowser's instruments are simple and light to handle, are in no way expensive, and require no power to operate them.

The subject of dowsing has never been explored fully by either the civil engineering or construction industries or their kindred professions. Dowsing has been heard about, and interesting stories have been told of remarkable finds forecast by experienced dowsers which have helped work on sites, and the news of these has even reached the press. But the subject is still looked upon with some suspicion mainly because it is considered to be an amateur pursuit with no link to science. Conditions are, however, starting to change as more people study dowsing and as more professional and technical specialists use it as an aid to their normal work; it is hoped that it may not be too long before the subject will be given a place in the regular curriculum of construction courses.

My anthology begins with the first article of the first issue of the *JBSD*, written in 1933, in which dowsing is studied from the medical viewpoint. This article, *The Cause of the Phenomena of Dowsing* by Dudley D'Auvergne Wright FRCS, makes one realise how little research on the causes behind dowsing has uncovered since that work was written, and his reasoning may well still be completely correct. The same is true of the research discussed in the article *The Physical Reactions of Dowsing* by Dr J.A. Simpson Emslie MB ChB, written in 1935. Much research work was done at this time by T. Bedford

Franklin and J. Cecil Maby BSc ARCS FRAS and was published in the various issues of the *Journal*. A look back at historical views is always interesting, and the article *Cornish Divining in 1808* by H.H. Langelaan describes the divining techniques of that time, and the attitudes towards them. As the article states, the rod was used to assist miners in their search for mineral lodes; dowsing was considered an aid which surpassed explanation, yet produced remarkable results.

Trained people, whether operatives or professionals, generally expect any aid to their work on site to have the support of orthodox learning and science. This is sound and logical enough, but because dowsing does not at present enjoy an easy explanation — this being due partly to its complex link with man's physiology — no real attempt has been made to date by a recognised research body to record findings and compare the known methods of dowsers and their reactions. The article *Prospecting by the Use of Science and Dowsing* by Dr A.R. Bailey BSc PhD MSc describes some comparative experiments of this kind carried out by him, and goes some way towards solving the problems of comparing man's senses with the findings of scientific survey instruments. This is interesting, encouraging, and the results are not unexpected.

The actual methods of using dowsing instruments to record the dowsing reaction have been described in detail in most of the classic dowsing handbooks. Some rare sensitives may say that they do not need to use any instrument, for they can feel the dowsing influence in their bare hands; some dowsers have even been known to 'see' the line of the dowsing reaction on the ground. But in most cases instruments and techniques to use them are required, and thus I have included several articles on these subjects in this anthology. The two articles on dowsing rods are in general self-explanatory; but no complete article on the pendulum and its characteristics has been published in the *Journal*, possibly because the subject is so well explained in the standard dowsing handbooks. A brief description of this instrument may thus not be amiss at this point.

A pendulum is a weight composed of any material — metal, wood, plastic, glass, natural stone, etc. — often pointed on the lower side and hung on a string, thread or chain. Generally the pendulum bob is about an inch or so long, and the thread length about 4″ — neither measurement is critical. The top end of the suspension thread is held by the thumb and forefinger of the right hand and the pendulum is allowed to swing freely over an object, or whatever is to be examined. Note is then taken if the pendulum starts to gyrate, clockwise or anti-clockwise, on its own, or swing in any compass direction. Much has been described in the *Journal* and in the handbooks on pendulum reactions, all of which may have some meaning to a dowser and may help him find an answer to his search.

A number of techniques and methods are used as aids in the dowsing process. Mention is made in a number of the articles to 'samples' techniques, so a short article on the subject is included, by the late Abbe Mermet. His classic book *Principles and Practice of Radiesthesia* (Stuart and Watkins, 1959) is well worth reading, as it covers very thoroughly the fundamentals of dowsing. Other techniques are described in the texts of two talks I gave to the Society, on *Colour in Dowsing* and *Proxy Dowsing*. The latter article describes an interesting method of dowsing which shows how the reaction sensed by the dowser can be varied and adapted to find information of use on site.

The most controversial subject in dowsing must be that of 'map dowsing', here described by Simon Stone in his article *One Map Dowsing Technique Explained*. To a non-dowser this subject may appear to be pure nonsense; but despite all the criticism the technique has great merits and — much to one's surprise and amazement — does seem to work and give sound results. No explanation as to how it operates appears to be convincing; the dowser seems to be functioning in a field of influence which modern scientific man cannot understand and finds very difficult to accept. I don't intend to explain here how map dowsing works or why it works, for I have no convincing answer; but I would state that I use map dowsing techniques when I undertake surveys of properties, and it has helped me greatly. In fact I have obtained answers to site problems from drawings and maps which have proved correct when investigations have been carried out later on the site. Accuracy may vary with different people, but I generally achieve about 70% correct forecasts. Map dowsing can save much time if carried out prior to a site survey, which is a great asset. Like other methods of dowsing, the subject of map dowsing is well described in many of the standard dowsing handbooks.

'Remanence' must be considered important when carrying out dowsing surveys of sites. Mistakes which are due to operating in an incorrect sequence are understandable; but when a clear indication is obtained of something which is simply not there, the puzzle starts. The phenomenon is described as remanence; generally the object has been removed earlier in time and seems to have left an image or shadow of its former self in its stead. The article *Beware of Ghosts* by H. Guttridge describes some of the pitfalls of this type, while *Notes for Beginners* by Col. Merrylees describes general approaches to dowsing practice in the field.

In the main collection of articles on site dowsing experiences which follow, I have tried to provide a wide cross section of applications of the art, giving many practical examples of answers to site problems commonly found to exist. As the articles show, all manner of things and conditions will respond to a dowsing search; but it must be borne in mind that a sound dowsing technique and preferably a specialised knowledge of the subject in which the search is being conducted will be a great advantage to a good dowser, in that he will judge his own findings far better and thus be able to give sound advice based on those findings.

I conclude this selection of articles with a lecture on *Why the Scientist Doubts the Dowser*, given by Dr D.M. Lewis MSc FIM. I do this for two reasons: firstly because I respect his opinion, and secondly I agree with his general advice on the need for a more methodical approach to dowsing practice and the recording of results. If more dowsers and people interested in dowsing do take his advice, perhaps better results would be obtained; if more scientists read this paper, perhaps they would decide it was about time dowsing was fully and properly researched; and then its real benefit would perhaps be recognised by all.

To conclude, a word of advice to those who may wish to carry out site surveys and dowsing work on construction sites. Do not expect ideal conditions, for sites are often wet, cold, muddy and littered with heaps of building materials and equipment. The site may have buildings or parts of buildings upon it, preventing the dowser from proceeding in a direction in which he wants to go. Some parts of a site may be inaccessible and may have steep slopes up which it is impossible to climb, or holes and diggings into which it is impossible to go. A clear clean level site is not a common occurrence! It must always be remembered that building and engineering operatives must not be prevented from working if at all possible, for time lost on site is expensive and the dowser will not be thanked if he disrupts building operations. When entering sites, always call at the site office first, for sites can be dangerous, especially when equipment is in use. With these warnings in mind, the survey must be conducted with responsibility; the dowser is advised to be proficient in the methods of dowsing checking one method against another wherever possible — the more checking the better — so no mistakes are made. An interesting method of checking one's dowsing is to carry out the work with one's eyes closed; it is surprising how an accurate 'feel' will develop and will prevent the dowser from 'reasoning' a result.

Clive Thompson

THE CAUSE OF THE PHENOMENA OF DOWSING
Dudley D'Auvergne Wright

THE question whether the phenomena of dowsing are to be attributed to physical, physiological or psychic causes has been fought out on many an arena. The protagonists for each theory have stoutly defended their own standpoint, and the result has usually been, that, after the clash of arms, each combatant has been found standing unmoved.

The Society for Psychical Research devoted a special number of its journal[1] to the discussion of this subject, the cudgels being taken up first by Vicomte Henry de France, whose comprehensive views on the subject are fairly well known through his book, which our President, Colonel Bell, has translated : *The Modern Dowser* (Bell & Sons Ltd.) ; secondly by Carl Graf von Klinckowström, a firm adherent of the physico-physiological School, who soundly trounces the worthy Vicomte and his compatriots M. Mager, the Abbés Bouly and Ferran, and many another noted French dowser who dare to draw conclusions from laboratory experiments, or what he calls ' armchair investigations ', indulge in the use of the pendulum, or endeavour to diagnose disease or estimate the yield of subterranean springs by means of the detector ; all of which he considers likely to bring obloquy on the art of dowsing.

Finally, Mr. Theodore Besterman enters the lists, and stoutly upholds the theory of Sir William Barrett, who in his work *The Divining Rod*, compiled by Mr. Besterman after the decease of its author, maintained that dowsing is a purely psychical process.

The writer of the present article does not wish to enter into this controversy, his object being to point out certain facts which in great part explain the action of the divining rod ; but before dealing with this, he would like to make a few remarks on the general position.

In the first place, it would seem that those who take an unprejudiced view of this matter can hardly exclude the idea of some psychical action. This appears to take place both in the conscious, as well as in the so-called subconscious realm. On the other hand, advocates of a purely psychical theory seem to overlook the presence of a physical medium connecting the psychism of the dowser with the object sought for (water, oil, metal, etc.). It is just this medium, be it ' radiations ', vibrations in the ether, or electricity, and its action upon the nervous system of the dowser, which bring the operation into the physico-

1

physiological domain.

Count von Klinckowström in his essay above mentioned says that the chief component of the process of dowsing is a physical stimulus of the nervous system of the dowser, and he quotes Dr. H. Haemel as saying that in the movements of the rod we are concerned with a system in labile tension represented by the hands and arms, separated by the dowsing rod, which can be easily brought out of equilibrium by any variations of the contractile state of the hand and arm musculature.

This is probably a correct explanation, and in this connection the following facts which appear to have been left out of account by those explaining the action of the rod, are of great importance :

As is well known, the nervous system is divided into the cerebro-spinal, and the involuntary (sympathetic) systems. So far as our muscles are concerned the cerebro-spinal system supplies them with nerves which convey only *voluntary impulses*. This at once rules out the cerebro-spinal system so far as the action of dowsing is concerned, for directly movements of a voluntary nature come into play, dowsing, which is essentially an involuntary process, is impossible.*

It is then only the involuntary nervous system, represented by the so-called sympathetic nerves, which can take a part in the act of dowsing, and it is in this connection that an important physiological point has been overlooked, viz., that every voluntary muscle of the body has a double nerve supply ; one from the cerebro-spinal system which conveys voluntary impulses, and another from the sympathetic nerves through which the tone of the muscle is regulated, and it is to this varying tone or tension of the muscle that we may attribute the movement of the rod.

There are other evidences that the sympathetic nervous system plays a large part in the phenomena associated with dowsing. For instance, it is no uncommon thing for those who are particularly sensitive to experience a sudden faintness and palpitation, or to show marked pallor of the face on passing into the zone of radiation from water, minerals, or other substances. This pallor is due to the contraction of the small blood vessels of the skin, which are under the control of the sympathetic nervous system.

Further phenomena can be adduced showing how sensitive the body is to the influence of certain substances at a distance. For instance, if a sensitive person be placed in a position facing

---

* The voluntary movements here referred to must be carefully distinguished from actions of the *will*, which subject is considered further on.

2

the west, a bright light be made to shine into the eye so as to contract the pupil, and a phial containing a drug to which the person has previously been shown to be sensitive is now brought close up to the back of the neck without the knowledge of the subject experimented on, a brief but very discernible dilation of the pupil will occur, and at the same time a slight acceleration of the pulse will often take place.

Both these actions are brought about through the sympathetic nervous system by reflex action. It can hardly be disputed that these reactions are all physico-physiological, and can partly be explained on the assumption that certain parts of the nervous system are concerned in their production.

Mr. Besterman in his article above referred to, in supporting the purely psychical theory, says that he need mention only one argument against the physical theory; viz., ' the complete absence of evidence for the existence in the human body of any organ capable of detecting, discriminating between, and measuring various electrical, magnetic, and/or radio-active currents, emanations or properties, and then communicating the result to the neuro-muscular system '. This statement is altogether too sweeping. There is evidence of the presence of an apparatus by which such emanations can be received and the necessary communication with the neuro-muscular system maintained.

There are at present in parts of the brain, the spinal cord, and especially in the sympathetic ganglia, certain large nerve cells which have a peculiar structure in that they possess at one end large branching processes much resembling the roots of trees, and at the other end are prolonged into a nerve fibre which passes away into the spinal cord, or into the nerves of the body.

The branches of one cell approach closely to, but do not actually touch, similar branches of a neighbouring cell. Moreover they are motile and capable of being retracted or extended under certain conditions. For instance, in the case of the brain, when sleep comes on it has been proved that these processes retract from each other so that the gap between them is much increased.

We thus have cells which are known to be conductors of electric currents, whose processes are in juxtaposition to and lying in a bed of matter which is a very poor conductor of electricity. Such a combination is to all intents and purposes a condenser such as we have in our wireless sets, and it is not unreasonable to assume that the action in both cases is similar,

3

viz., that of 'tuning in' to the different wave-lengths and frequencies through a variation of capacity.

Furthermore, in the nuclei of the cells of the body we have structures which are capable of 'inductance'. They are the so-called chromosomes, which are coiled, tubular threads having an outer coat made of a fat-like insulating substance, containing a fluid with mineral salts in solution forming a liquid of high electrical conductivity. Lakhovsky[2] asserts that these structures are electro-magnetic oscillators, and that since they vary in size and curvature they all differ in the length of wave to which they are capable of oscillating.

We thus have in the body two distinct contrivances which are capable of varying degrees of inductance and capacity, both of which are in direct relationship with the nervous system. The whole is linked up in what is called in physiological language, a reflex arc ; which consists of a receiving apparatus—in this case the skin; a centrally transmitting apparatus—the centripetally directed nerves from the skin ; a central receiving station—the large nerve cells which are capable of 'tuning in' to the various wave-lengths received ; from this again the impulse is transmitted through the sympathetic nerves to the muscle fibres of the arm and fingers which hold the divining rod, and through this impulse, variations in the tension of the muscle are produced, and a turning of the detector thereby brought about.

All the above activities take place in the lower and more primitive part of the nervous system and are of a subconscious nature, the brain itself taking no conscious part in the action. But it would seem that in certain cases it is not possible to exclude the higher faculties of the brain from a share in the transaction, and it is here that a psychic factor enters in.

It is generally conceded by expert water diviners that by an effort of concentration and will power, it is possible to tune the receptive system into—shall we say—the wave-length of any particular substance, be it gold, oil, water, etc.

In Sir Wm. Barrett's book, *The Divining Rod*[3], the following will be found as the evidence given by the Rev. H. J. T. Tringham of Long Cross Vicarage, Chertsey, who is evidently a dowser of considerable sensitiveness ; ' Last night I was making the test (by dowsing) over a lot of coins—silver and copper, and the rod moved in a lively fashion, but I found . . . that it would only work if the thought of metal was in my mind. If I thought of water it would not work for metal, and vice versa. Well, that is weird enough, but it occurred to me that I might be deceiving

4

myself as to the movement of the rod over the coins, more especially when I found that to get it to operate I had to think of the particular metal of which the coins were made! So I devised a test. I made parcels of silver coins and parcels of copper coins, and " jumbled " them up together so that I had not the least idea which metal any one of them contained. Then I selected one at hazard, put it on the floor and tried the rod over it, thinking of silver. " Nothing doing ", as the boys say. Changed my thought to copper, and the rod moved. Copper it was ! I tried each packet in turn and the rod never made a mistake ! This is rather uncanny, but fascinating. I tried with pewter, and with an ordinary tin and got no result.'

Other instances of a similar nature could be quoted, and so it appears that man has a selective control over the actions of dowsing, and it is to that extent a psychological process ; but in all instances the greater part of the procedure must be ascribed to a physico-physiological action.

Continental dowsers are now generally recognizing that not only is their art closely allied to wireless on the one hand, but that the reactions of which the dowsing rod or detector gives evidence are essentially the same as the so-called electronic reactions of Abrams.

The latter have in the past been so decried by the many leaders of the medical profession in spite of the able advocacy of Sir James Barr that it will be some consolation and satisfaction to those who use them for medical purposes, to find support for their methods from workers in another field.

There can be little doubt that the reactions taking place in the human ' reagent ' in Abrams method are brought about by the same physiological train of actions as is the case with the dowser.

A further extension with the dowsing rod has taken place in the domain of medicine of late. It has been found by several observers that by means of the use of ' samples ' it is possible to detect the presence of morbid germs in the living bodies of man and animal.

The University of Paris has lately conferred the degree of Doctor of Veterinary Medicine on Dr. Abel Martin for a thesis on the use of the pendulum in the diagnosis of animal maladies.[4] In this thesis numerous illustrations of the diagnosis of disease in cattle, horses and sheep caused by microbes and food poisoning are given.

His methods were very severely put to the test by a jury of

three veterinary experts, the object of the investigation being to discover by means of the pendulum the number of cows—out of a total of forty—that were affected with tuberculosis. Previous to the experiment the animals had been tested by the tuberculin reaction method, the result being unknown to Dr. Martin. Out of the total of forty the pendulum showed thirty-nine to have tubercle in some form. The tuberculin test gave 38, but there was reason to suspect that the thirty-ninth cow did not respond to the tuberculin test for certain reasons which we need not enter into. The tests were carried out under conditions most unfavourable to the doctor, and the result obtained was certainly highly creditable.

A still further use of the rod has been found in the selection of suitable foods and remedies in the treatment of disease. The subject is one which has only lately been brought forward, and there are not a large number of workers in these lines yet, and it would be best to leave the consideration of this subject to a later date.

Since the above was written there has appeared in the Guy's Hospital Gazette for June 24th, 1933, a most important article by Dr. Lintott entitled ' Some Observations on So-called Water Divining '. The article is based upon a series of experiments undertaken in the Physiological department of Guy's Hospital, and out in the country. In the former case an apparatus was constructed so that water might run in a pipe beneath a platform, but without the knowledge and sight of the observer. What adds particular value to this investigation is that, as Dr. Lintott emphasises, all the experiments were carried out in a strong spirit of scepticism and under critical observation, and, where possible, control experiments were made.

It is only possible to summarise the results. They are briefly as follows : It was found that whereas no person tested could detect the presence of still water, yet there were people who possessed sensitivity to moving water to a varying degree. These persons could be classified in three groups :

1. Those completely insensitive.
2. Those in whom the sensitivity was present but not marked, and in whom it varied from time to time, being most evident when they were in a state of physical well-being.
3. Those in whom marked sensitivity was constantly present.

The twig and rods simply act as indicators and also as the means whereby the correct state of muscular tension is achieved. Three factors are thought to be concerned in the production of the response—a stimulus, the nature of which is unknown and which emanates from running water ; a receptive organ in the body, the sensitivity of which seems to be intimately connected with muscle tone ; and, lastly, the motor force which results in movement of the indicator used, and this, it appears, is a change of tone in the muscles of the hands and forearms.

It is interesting to note that its author comes to the same conclusions as expressed in this article as to the movement of the rod being due to alterations in the tension of the dowser's muscles. A further proof that increased tension of probably all the muscles of the body is caused by the action of running water is given by the experiment of making the dowser hold a rubber bulb in his mouth, and bite it lightly so as to secure the necessary tension. The bulb was connected by means of a tube with a tracing needle and recording drum so that any alterations in the tension would be registered by the tracing needle. As soon as the dowser walked over the pipe containing the running water a tracing was obtained which showed an increase of tension in the jaw muscles at the exact point that the dowser passed over the water. It was also proved that blindfolding made no difference to the manifestation of the phenomena of dowsing, but a considerable proportion of errors occurred when the attention of the dowser was distracted whilst he was operating. This points to some action of the higher cerebral centres and may be related to the function of ' tuning in ' by a conscious selective action of the dowser such as has been referred to in an earlier page.

The article itself is full of interesting points raised by the experiments performed, and should be read by all who are interested in the subject.

It is a matter of supreme importance to the dowsing fraternity that the subject has now been investigated in a truly scientific way by a recognized authority, and that further investigations are to be made ; and it is a matter of the greatest satisfaction that the main propositions of dowsers have been so far confirmed by the investigations.

Bibliography.
   [1] Journal of the Society for Psychical Research No. 479, Vol. xxvii, Nov. 1931.
   [2] *La Formation Néoplastique et les déséquilibre oscillatoire cellulaire* : S. Doin, Paris.
   [3] *The Divining Rod*, Sir William Barrett & Theodore Besterman : Methuen.
   [4] Published as *Diagnostic Radiesthésique en Médecine-Vétérinaire :* Librairie Le François, Paris.

THE PHYSICAL REACTIONS OF DOWSING

Dr J.A. Simpson Emslie

I am sure that to all of us dowsing is a very interesting, complex and mysterious subject. At the present time there is a great deal of controversy as to the cause of the phenomena that occur in the human body. There are two main schools of thought, and they are both hypothetical. First, there are those who believe that radiations occur, not only from living things, such as plants and animals, but from inanimate objects as well, such as water, minerals and stone, and, in fact, anything that you care to mention. They believe that these radiations are picked up by the dowser who is susceptible to them.

The other school of thought hold that phenomena are produced by psychic causes, and are associated with telepathy and clairvoyance. Whatever the cause, however, the reactions as they occur in the human body are well defined, and here we are treading on more certain ground. A knowledge of both Anatomy and Physiology help us. We can study the physical movements which take place—these are the movements of the rod and also the pendulum, and a knowledge of physiology explains why these movements occur in the way they do.

In talking to many dowsers and also in reading articles in the Journal, I find that there is a great diversity of opinion as to how the movements occur and also regarding the actual movements themselves. This, unfortunately, tends to still further complicate an already complex subject, and it is my intention this afternoon to put before you certain facts and observations which, I think, will tend to simplify and explain these physical reactions.

REFLEX ACTION.

Now in the first place it is obvious that a muscular movement takes place, whether we use the rod or whether we use the pendulum. In the case of the rod, when it moves upward you find that the hands are also flexing at the wrist, and when the pendulum is used you find the whole arm is moving slightly, giving the pendulum its circular movement.

Now, we ask ourselves, what type of movement is this ? Is it a voluntary movement or is it involuntary ? The answer to that is, that it is undoubtedly involuntary. One means by that that it is not under the control of the will. We do not put the rod up consciously, the movements of the muscles which take place come on by their own accord. This involuntary movement is known as reflex action.

Now I will give you a few examples of what reflex action is. If I cross one leg over the other and let it hang loose and give a sharp tap below the kneecap, my leg springs forward. Medically this is known as the knee-jerk. Here involuntary muscular action has taken place causing the muscles above the knee to contract, with the result that the leg extends. Again, if somebody lightly scratches the sole of the foot you draw your leg up. The same applies if, unconsciously, you put your hand on something very hot. Your hand is withdrawn before you have had time to realise what has happened.

There are many other types of reflex action ; yawning, sneezing and coughing are all reflex. If a crumb of bread goes down the " wrong way " a contraction of your windpipe takes place and severe coughing follows, which you are unable to control, and it is absolutely involuntary. Now the reactions in dowsing are exactly the same as this. We first have a stimulus, such as the tap below the knee, the scratching of the sole of the foot or the crumb of bread in the windpipe. A message is conveyed up a set of nerves to the spinal cord and from there the stimulus passes down another set of nerves—the motor nerves—to the muscles which cause the movements such as I have described.

Now in dowsing, say we are looking for a well, is it not possible that the water is the stimulus and the action of our hands is the muscular reflex response ? I think there is no question that it is.

There is another very important physiological fact, and that is that the brain controls these reflexes—it inhibits them. If there was no brain-control these reflexes would act most severely, and the slightest stimulus would set them off. In fact, if there was no control, by tickling the sole of the foot the whole leg would be drawn up, and it would go into a spasm which would remain for some time.

Nature provides for this control by nerves from the brain to the spinal cord to meet the various reflex arcs occurring below. Now, as you can understand, if these nerves from the brain to the spinal cord are damaged, either by injury or disease, the reflexes which are controlled by them will immediately become very exaggerated if they are stimulated. Clinically this is what we do find.

Diseases such a cerebral hæmorrhage or " shock," injury to the brain, and many nerve diseases destroy these nerves, and we get our greatly increased reflex action.

If we wish, therefore, to prove that the physical reactions of dowsing are reflex, what we have to do, is to get a person suffering from one of these diseases and see what happens. They should be extraordinarily good dowsers from the point of view of reaction.

I have been very fortunate in seeing two cases ; both were in a way similar, having had small cerebral hæmorrhages, presumably caused during birth. The last case I came across was at our Inch-

9

marlo meeting in July, and I was able to demonstrate his extraordinary reactions to some of the members, including our President.

When this man was using the rod his reactions were so severe as to practically throw him into a spasm. In his case he was affected on one side more than the other, with the result that this side acted very much more, and he told me, on occasions, the reaction was sufficient to make him lose his balance and he would fall to the ground. When dowsing, his arm, leg and muscles of the face were all contracted on the affected side. This, indeed, therefore, is proof that the reactions of dowsing are reflex. I have something more to mention about this man when we consider the movements of the pendulum.

Now, as I have said, the brain controls these reflexes to a very large extent, so that it would seem that in dowsing what we actually do is to take off our mental control. It is in a way the exact opposite of voluntary will. We do not inhibit our reflexes so much, so that they become more sensitive.

It is a curious fact that there are certain emotional states which do the same thing, such as fear. When we are in that condition we start and jump at the slightest noise and our heart goes racing, which means that our mental control is lessened. These emotional states leave us rather exhausted and pale, and it is well known that many dowsers experience the same symptoms after dowsing for any length of time.

I think there is no doubt our sympathetic nervous system is markedly affected. The palor which is produced in the face is caused by contraction of the blood vessels of the skin, and this is entirely under the control of the sympathetic system. It is quite possible then that we may get other symptoms such as headache and a rise in the pulse rate as some have noted, but I do not think these symptoms would manifest themselves until the dowser began to show signs of fatigue.

THE ROD.

First let me say that the rod is nothing more or less than an indicator of muscular movement. The material of which the rod is made matters not the slightest. Its shape, however, is important.

Many have the idea that the rod must be made of some wood or material which has an affinity for water, such as willow, hazel or broom, but we know that we can find it with any type of rod—steel wires or whalebone, and, in fact, it is not necessary to use a rod at all. By flexing the fingers slightly you will find that in passing over water flexion takes place at the wrist and so the hands move in an upward direction.

Another erroneous idea is that there is an electrical current passing along the rod, and one hears of dowsers talking of positive and negative poles or potentials. This, of course, is quite

10

impossible, as many of the rods are non-conductors of electricity.
Some have specially coloured rods and materials in the rod
itself. These can be of no value; the only value they may have
is to help the dowser to concentrate on what he is finding.

The V shape of the rod, however, is of importance. As we
hold it in our hands it acts as a spring, and in this way it will
exaggerate the very smallest muscular movement. Therefore
the more spring the rod has the better. That is why whalebone
is so very good and is used by many.

There is another factor here, and that is, by holding the rod
one has to flex the fingers, and in this way tone is put in the
flexor muscles. It is known that a reflex will act more easily
if there is already tone in the muscles.

By using the rod we are only indicating movement in the
flexor muscles of the forearm. Now it should be possible to
indicate movement in any muscle we care to choose, as long as
we take our mental control off it and allow the reflex to take
place, and this is what we do find.

By holding the arms well out and putting tone in the extensor
muscles of the arm and thinking of the extensors, you will find
that the rod will tend to move down, although this is a difficult
movement to carry out because extension is limited. This
can also be demonstrated even with the tongue, if it is held mid-
way between the roof and floor of the mouth. You will find
that the reaction will make it rise towards the palate. Again,
this was also shown by an experiment on the massetter muscle
of the jaw. This experiment was carried out by Dr. Lintott,
in Guy's Hospital, when he made patients bite on a rubber ball
and the movement of the massetter muscle was thereby conveyed
to an instrument which registered the contraction.

I now believe that everybody is a potential dowser, and that
it is not a gift which is given to only a few. I have in many
instances been able to make people dowse who could not do it at
all before and it was no " influence " of mine which was conveyed to them, but simply an explanation of how to relax their
muscles and allow the reflex to occur.

One of the main reasons why so many people fail is that they
hold the rod so firmly in their hands, with the wrists fixed, both
their flexors and extensors being contracted, that it is absolutely
impossible for any movement to occur. Once they are able to
stop concentrating on the rod and are able to concentrate on the
water and keep their wrists slack, then they find that an involuntary movement will take place.

Just before I leave the rod there is another very important
point I wish to mention. Many dowsers say that the rod turns
down and others say it turns up when they are over water. Some
dowsers may find it turns up for one thing and down for another.

I am now going to tell you that that, in my opinion, is of no importance whatever. It depends entirely on how you hold the rod. The muscular movement is the same in both cases—that of flexion.

I have studied a large number of dowsers on this point, and in those who got a downward movement I was able to get the opposite by making them hold the point of the rod slightly higher, and in all cases I noted the reaction was really flexion. It is very easy to make the rod go down, particularly if you hold the point of the rod slightly below the horizontal. You may ask, why does it always go down for one substance ? My answer to that is that unconsciously it is very easy to make the rod go down, particularly if you know the substance you are reacting to, but it is flexion that has occurred all the same.

Now, briefly, I will say a few words about the pendulum.

THE PENDULUM.

The circular movement that takes place is also due to reflex muscular movement. If you watch a person dowsing with this instrument you will note that the whole arm is imparting the movement. Anything in the nature of a pendulum will do—a key, a ball, or a ring attached to a piece of string. Like the rod, it does not matter what is used. Its action is only showing up a muscular movement.

Now here the reflex action appears to be somewhat different from that of the rod, in that its movement is a rhythm and it is this action which causes the pendulum to gyrate. If held in the right hand the action is clockwise—the same direction that one normally uses when stirring anything—and if held in the left hand the motion is anti-clockwise, which is to be expected seeing that we are using the exact opposite set of muscles. I believe the rhythm is quite a normal one, and I am quite sure that many of you will have noticed that, on occasions, when you have been sitting on a chair with your feet on the floor, that a jerking, rhythmic movement takes place when you raise your heels off the ground. The condition called " clonus," known to medical men, is just an exaggeration of this movement, and it occurs in those patients as I mentioned before who have had the mental control of their reflexes cut off. I was able to demonstrate a well-marked clonus on the dowser at Inchmarlo of whom I spoke before. It was very easily produced on slightly bending his knee and jerking his foot upwards. On doing so a rhythmic movement commenced at the ankle and this continued as long as I kept pressure on the toes.

On the first case of this type that I examined I was fortunate in being able to demonstrate a clonus in the dowser's arms as he held the rod, so that I am quite sure that a small rhythmic movement occurs in the arms when we use the rod, but it is so small that it is difficult to see or demonstrate. Now all this goes to prove that no matter what instrument we use our physical reactions are the same.

There is a point I might mention here, and that is the action of a dowser on another person. If a novice is trying to use the pendulum with no success and a dowser places his hand on the arm holding the pendulum, gyration very often takes place, and it is thought some " influence " has passed from the dowser into the novice. This is not the case. What has really happened is that the dowser's own movements are communicated indirectly to the pendulum. The same applies to the rod. If the dowser holds one end of the rod and a novice the other, the dowser's upward movement will give the impression to the novice that he now can do it because his end will also tend to move up, whether he tries to hold it down or not. I am sure you will all have seen this done.

And now, in conclusion, I will just summarise the principal points in this address.

CONCLUSIONS.

(1). All instruments used in dowsing are to indicate muscular movement.

(2). The muscular movement is involuntary and is reflex action

(3). The brain controls the reflexes and in dowsing we take off that control.

As I have mentioned, everybody is a potential dowser, and with a little knowledge and practice they can become successful. The more often one dowses the easier does it become. Errors, unfortunately, are very easily produced, mental suggestion being one of the worst to catch the unwary.

If one imagines that water should be present, then perhaps one will react whether it is there or not. A person who can concentrate well, and whose mind is not influenced by suggestion will be an accurate dowser.

CORNISH DIVINING IN 1808
H.H. Langelaan

I have just been re-reading one of my treasured books : *A Tour through Cornwall in the Autumn of 1808*, by the Revd. Richard Warner, published in 1809. Towards the end of his delightful description of the tour, the Author dwells awhile on the subject of Divining.

He mentions that he fully expected to find among the miners of Cornwall many superstitious notions, but the only remnants of superstition which he discovered amongst them were "a careful abstaining from *whistling* when underground, and a firm belief in the efficacy of the *Virgula Divinitoria*, or Divining Rod."

He agreed that the virtues of the Divining Rod were acknowledged by other miners besides those of Cornwall, for he had heard them positively asserted among the miners employed in the *lapis calaminaris* mines of Mendip. Those miners, he said, " would as soon as doubted the power of gunpowder in blasting the rock, as the influence of this magical wand in pointing out the invisible course of mineral veins." The Author gave us a glimpse of his own disbelief when he continued : " It must be observed, however, that implicit credit is not given to the virtue of the Virgula by *all* the persons concerned in the Cornish mines : most of the workmen are firm believers in it ; but many of the captains are sceptical ; and all the proprietors absolute infidels in this respect."

How much those remarks remind us of the saying that " human nature does not change." The reluctance of the overseers, and the refusal of the proprietors to believe the evidence of the working of a human faculty, seems to demonstrate the action of the superiority complex in those days, just as in these times the Medical profession appears to exhibit the same psychological attitude towards clairvoyant diagnosis.

The Author stated that the Divining Rod was introduced into this country during Queen Anne's reign by a Spaniard, named Captain Ribeira, who deserted from the service of his own country, and was made Captain Commandant of the garrison of Plymouth. " The efficacy which it appeared to possess in his hands made it a popular instrument in all the English mining counties, and as *implicit faith* accompanied its use, so those accidental discoveries which it was impossible should *not* occasionally occur in districts intersected by lodes, to persons who tried the country with it, served to increase its credit ; while the disappointments or mistakes which more frequently attended its operations, were ever put to the account of the Virgula being irregularly made, improperly held, or the person carrying it not being one in whose hands it would act."

Who can resist a smile at such an ingenious argument ? What an ornament was lost to the legal profession when the Author chose the Church. He gives due credit, however, to Pryce, whom he describes as one of the most scientific and experienced miners in Cornwall ; and I believe I can do no better than give his quotations from Pryce's account of the construction and use of the rod.

" The rods formerly used were shoots of one year's growth that grew forked ; but it is found that two separate shoots tied together with some vegetable substance, as pack thread, will

14

answer rather better than those which are green forked, as their shoots being seldom of equal length or bigness they do not handle so well as the others, which may be chosen of the same size. The shape of the rod thus prepared will be between two and a half and three feet long. They must be tied together at their great or root ends, the smaller being to be held in the hands. Hazel rods cut in the winter, such as are used for fishing rods, and kept till they are dry, do best ; though where these are not at hand, apple-tree suckers, rods from peach trees, currants, or the oak, though green, will answer tolerably well."

" It is very difficult to describe the manner of holding and using the rod ; it ought to be held in the hands, the smaller ends lying flat or parallel to the horizon, and the upper part in an elevation not perpendicular to it, but seventy degrees."

" The rod being properly held by those with whom it will answer, when the toe of the right foot is within the semi-diameter of the piece of metal or other subject of the rod, it will be repelled towards the face, and continue to be so, while the foot is kept from touching or being directly over the subject ; in which case, it will be sensibly and strongly attracted, and be drawn quite down. The rod should be firmly and steadily grasped ; for if, when it hath begun to be attracted there be the least imaginable jerk, or opposition to its attraction, it will not move any more, till the hands are opened and a fresh grasp taken. The stronger the grasp, the livelier the rod moves, provided the grasp be steady, and of an equal strength. This observation is very necessary, as the operation of the rod in many hands is defeated purely by a jerk or counter action ; and it is from thence concluded, there is no real efficacy in the rod, or that the person who holds it wants the virtue ; whereas by a proper attention to this circumstance in using it, five persons in six have the virtue as it is called ; that is, the nut or fruit bearing rod will answer in their hands. When the rod is drawn down, the hands must be opened, the rod raised by the middle fingers, a fresh grasp taken, and the rod held again in the direction described."

" A little practice by a person in earnest about it, will soon give him the necessary adroitness in the use of this instrument ; but it must be particularly observed, that as our animal spirits are necessary to this process, so a man ought to hold the rod with the same indifference and inattention to, or reasoning about it, or its effects, as he holds a fishing-rod or walking-stick ; for if the mind be occupied by doubts, reasoning, or any other operation that engages the animal spirits, it will divert their powers from being exerted in this process, in which their instrumentality is absolutely necessary ; from hence it is that the rod constantly answers in the hands of peasants, women and children, who hold it simply without puzzling their minds with doubts or reasonings. Whatever may be thought of this observation, it is a very just one, and of great consequence in the practice of the rod."

" If a rod, or the least piece of one, of the nut-bearing or fruit kind, be put under the arm, it will totally destroy the operation of the Virgula Divinatoria in regard to all the subject of it, except water, in those hands in which the rod naturally operates. If the least animal thread, as silk, or worsted, or hair, be tied round or fixed on the top of the rod, it will in like manner hinder its operation ; but the same rod placed under the arm, or the same animal substance tied round or fixed on the top of the rod, will make it work in those hands, in which, without these additions, it is not attracted.

" The willow, and other rods, that will not answer in the hands in which the fruit or nut bearing rods attracted, will answer in those hands in which the others will not ; so that all persons using suitable rods in a proper manner have the virtue as it is called of the rod. A piece of the same willow placed under the arm, or the silk, worsted or hair, bound round, or fixed to the top of it, will make it answer with those to whom the nut or fruit bearing rods are naturally suitable, and in whose hands, without those additions, it would not answer."

" All rods, in all hands, answer to springs of water."

" If a rod is wanted for distinguishing copper or gold, procure filings of iron, lead, and tin, some leaf silver, chalk in powder, coal in powder, and rasped bones : let a hole be bored with a small gimlet in the top of the rod ; then mix the least imaginable quantity of the above ingredients, and put it in the gimlet hole with a peg of the same wood with the rod ; when it will only be attracted by what is left out, viz., gold and copper."

" In preparing the rod for distinguishing the white metals, leave out the lead, tin, and leaf silver, and add copper filings to the other ingredients ; and so of every subject by which you would have the rod attracted, the respective filings or powder must be left out of the mixture which is to be put into the hole at the top of the rod. As for coal and bones, they may be omitted in the distinguishing rods that are used in Cornwall, for obvious reasons : but it is necessary to put in the chalk or lime ; for though there is no limestone in the mining parts of the county, yet there are abundance of strata that draw the rod as limestone ; for the distinction of a dead or a live course, holds as well in regard to limestone, as to metals. This, however paradoxial it may appear, is a truth easily to be proved ; and it is one axiom in the science of the rod, that it makes no distinction between the living and dead parts of a course. Like the lodestone, it only shows the course, leaving the success of the undertaking to the fortune, skill, and management of the

16

miner ; as the lodestone doth that of the voyage, to the fortune, ability, and prudence of the mariner and merchant."

" The rod being guarded against all subjects except that which you want to discover, as tin and copper, for example ; walk steadily and slowly on with it ; and a person that hath been accustomed to carry it, will meet with a single repulsion and attraction, every three, four, and five yards, which must not be heeded, it being only from the water that is between every bed of killas, grouan, or other strata.   When the holder approaches a lode so near as its semi-diameter, the rod feels loose in the hands, and is very sensibly repelled towards the face ; if it be thrown back so far as to touch the hat, it must be brought forward to its usual elevation, when it will continue to be repelled till the foremost foot is over the edge of the lode : when this is the case, if the rod is held well, there will first be a small repulsion towards the face ; but this is momentary ; and the rod will be immediately drawn irresistibly down, and will continue to do so in the whole passage over the lode ; but as soon as the foremost foot is beyond its limits, the attraction from the hindmost foot, which is still on the lode, or else the repulsion on the other side, or both, throw the rod back towards the face.   The distance from the point where the attraction begun, and where it ended, is the breadth of the lode ; or rather a horizontal section of the bryle or back just under the earth.   We must then turn, and trace it on obliquely, or in the way of zig-zag, as far as may be thought necessary."

" In the course of this tracing a lode, all the circumstances of it, so far as they relate to its back, will be discovered ; as its breadth at different places, its being squeezed together by hard strata, its being cut off and thrown aside from its regular course by a cross-gossan, &c."

After this lengthy and interesting quotation from Pryce, the Author reveals himself again in this comment : " We were told, it is true, many stories to confirm the above surprizing accounts of the powers of the *Virgula Divinatoria ;* but none of them were of sufficient weight to make us converts to a faith in its virtues ; and we came away from our informants in much the same temper of mind as Johnson left the reporters of the *second sight* faculty, rather willing to believe, than actually convinced that what we had heard had any foundation in truth." Truly has it been said : " A man convinced against his will, is of the same opinion still."

PROSPECTING BY THE USE OF SCIENCE AND DOWSING

Dr Arthur Bailey

When prospecting for water, metallic ores or other features such as archæological sites, there are several methods available. The first and most obvious is sight. In a considerable number of cases the presence of old burial sites, buildings or outcropping ores can be located by aerial photographs, or even direct viewing when the sun is low in the sky. Such obvious methods will not be mentioned any further as they are very limited in their application.

In the absence of visual clues, then more sophisticated methods must be employed. On the physical plane, these are mainly electrical and magnetic. The most common method used is that of measuring the electrical resistance of the ground. This resistance is low where there is a high mineral or humus level that rises to high values in regions of rock and shale. An underground ditch can therefore be located by the resistance values falling sharply in the area immediately over the ditch. Similarly old stone foundations will show up as a rising value as compared with that of the surroundings. Nevertheless on waterlogged sites and sites that have been extremely cultivated or built on the results can be very difficult to interpret.

Another commonly used method is based on the small distortions produced in the earth's magnetic field by materials such as stone and soil and metallic ores. The instrument used is called a magnetometer and has to be very sensitive in order to measure changes of less than one part in ten thousand. For this reason magnetometers are very expensive and can cost as much as several thousand pounds. The results obtained by magnetometer surveys can be very good, and this is beoming the favourite method for site surveying. Nevertheless mistakes can be made, and one site was excavated in the East Riding of Yorkshire on very slender magnetometer results. In fact the magnetic anomaly was natural in the rock, and not due to a chariot burial as had been hoped. If a dowser had made the same mistake he would have been severely criticised, but needless to say magnetometers were not criticised for this reason. In fact the correct view was taken in that no surveying technique is infallible. It is a pity that dowsers cannot be accorded a similar margin for error.

A rather less common method of surveying is to measure the magnetic properties of the soil without using the earth's magnetic field as a reference. This method tends to be restricted to shallow depths but does enable one to detect metal objects and often can indicate whether the metal is iron or non-ferrous such as copper or brass. An instrument of this type developed by the

18

author has been used successfully to locate a suspected mediæval pottery kiln and also located on the same site two iron rods, an old sickle blade and a brass buckle. This latter object could not have been located by any other method of instrumentation.

At the University of Bradford we have a small group working on comparisons between the different surveying techniques, and as the main interest was archæology, I suggested using dowsing as a technique. Archæology has distinct advantages for such surveying comparisons, as the sites chosen are normally excavated soon afterwards and enable accurate conclusions and comparisons to be made.

The first site I was involved with is in the East Riding at Burton Fleming. I asked for a sketch of the site and knew of no other details whatever. My wife, sister-in-law and myself then spent an evening map dowsing and finished up with spots marked all over the map but particularly near to the gate in the field. Several weeks later I went to the site and did a survey without reference to the map. Marker pegs were put in wherever a reaction was obtained. Again the majority were near to the gate, but one set traced out an obvious straight line. Soil resistivity measurements were then taken, and surely enough they hit a maximum value over the marker pegs. In fact I had located the edge of an ancient barrow site. Where the scatter of pegs was near the gate, the resistance readings fluctuated wildly; and where little reaction had been obtained the readings kept pretty well constant.

In the map dowsing, one area in particular responded to human remains, pottery and iron and bronze. It was therefore very encouraging to see that when excavated the majority of the finds were in the areas indicated by dowsing, and indeed all the predicted substances were found in the areas mentioned.

It must be noted that I was given no clue as to what might be found on the site at any stage until the dowsing was finished. This was done personally so as to remove all possibility of auto suggestion.

The next site examined was at Castle Hill, near Huddersfield, and this proved to be a marathon event. The main site is an Iron Age hill fort that has been later built on by the Normans. One area in particular was decided on for investigation and this was dowsed over and checked for soil resistivity. The results were then plotted and checked one against the other. They show a very marked degree of similarity, maximum dowsing reaction tending to be obtained where the soil resistance changes most rapidly. Unfortunately the whole site was not excavated, but the excavation results showed that the majority of " finds " were where indicated by the dowsing survey.

On the same site there is a mysterious shaft about eight feet square that is driven directly down into the bed rock. It was known that it had been excavated to about thirty-five feet in the past without finding the bottom. It had then been filled in for safety. This shaft was to be excavated last year so it was dowsed on site and from a map before operations commenced. The result was the rather improbable figure of one hundred and five feet, give or take five feet or so. The final depth reached last year was about sixty-eight feet with the shaft still going down. The debris out of the shaft is Norman, showing that the shaft must be older than that.

All being well it is hoped to excavate further this year, so it will be interesting to see what results. I also got indications of a tunnel running radially outwards from the base of the shaft towards the site of some ruined cottages. I got indications that this is largely collapsed so I am waiting with interest for digging to be resumed.

For the dowsing surveys the instruments used were the author and angle rods. Angle rods were used as they give a rapid answer that is regularily categorised into weak, medium, strong and very strong. For the map dowsing a pendulum was used and in all cases analysis was on a question needing " yes " or " no " answer basis.

Certainly at the present state of the art, physical prospecting techniques are not infallible and frequently are very difficult to interpret. Underground streams at any reasonable depth are very difficult if not impossible to locate and any estimate of yield is out of the question. I therefore feel that physical and dowsing methods are complementary, and there is no question that it is far less tiring to do a quick map dowse over a prospective site than tramp all over it with surveying instruments.

Given that the results obtained between physical and dowsing methods do correlate, is there then any link between the two? My own personal view is that the link is not obvious at the moment and we may well be evaluating by dowsing on a completely different basis. Certainly time and distance do not enter into dowsing in the normal way, and perhaps this gives us the clue.

Experiments have been made with both dowsers and clairvoyants under conditions where any electromagnetic radiation theories could not have worked but yet they were still successful. If it is not electromagnetic radiation, how about magnetism? Again tests have shown that magnetic screens have no effect so that is another non starter. The truth appears to be that dowsing cannot be explained on a basis of physical theory as we understand it at the moment. It may be *convenient* to think of it in terms of radiation, but what type of radiation it is and at what frequency it is radiated no one seems to know. One can talk

20

about flow fields and reflection patterns and such and give the subject an apparent air of pure science, but when one appreciates that many dowsers do not react to these supposed patterns and knowing the powers of auto-suggestion one must be very careful before becoming dogmatic. Certainly it would need very carefully phased experiments with absolute newcomers to dowsing to establish the reality of such patterns.

For an experiment I once announced to myself that my angle rods would move outwards over an anomaly rather than their usual inward swing for me. As expected, the rods then proceeded to indicate in reverse of their usual direction. Equally I can pick up a pattern of seven influences on each side of a stream (but only after reading Mermet's book) I can however get a pattern of six or five or whatever number I choose merely by telling myself that that is what I expect to get. I normally use seven as being convenient but I am not at all certain that it is a basic law.

As dowsers in a somewhat antagonistic scientific world, we must avoid becoming too dogmatic about what we class as fundamentals of dowsing. The main thing is to find a method that works well for yourself and stick to it. There should be no need to bolster ourselves with pseudo-science and it is very dangerous as it can be exploded so easily by those with a mind to do so—who, then, state to the world at large that they have proved dowsing to be a myth!

No, dowsing can stand very well on its own feet purely on the results that can be obtained from it. As a surveying technique I have found it to be very useful and correlate well with other methods and what is actually found on excavation. I still believe, however, that it is far better to be honest and say " it works, although I must confess I don't fully understand it.'' I normally add that I am trying to find out more about it—which I am—but I find that this approach gives any opposition little to argue about but the actual evidence for dowsing, which as I said before is all that is necessary to justify the reality and use of dowsing.

DOWSING RODS

Clive Thompson

In this complex subject it is quite possible to find oneself in agreement with some people and in disagreement with others. The dowsing phenomenon has defied experts being able to give a convincing reason for its workings and results, but this does not imply that there is no answer and that it will never be found. The facts of dowsing are far too convincing for any reasoning person to dismiss them as sheer fantasy. I feel it is the duty of

21

this Society to spare no effort to try to unlock the secret that has teased man during the centuries that he has been divining and getting what appeared to be the " magic " result.

There are basically two schools of thought: One believes the rod only is affected by the dowsing forces and twists over a reaction, the other believes that the natural physical force fields of influence that emanate from matter are picked up by the nervous centres of the body, transmitted to the brain, and a resultant neuro-muscular action is given to the arms. The muscles in the arms and fingers are so affected that a reflex condition occurs, which triggers off the near-balanced position of dowsing rods; these rods being so held that, if disturbed from the standard hold, a collapsed form occurs in their shape. Alternatively, the rod may be so held that it amplifies involuntary muscular action stimulated by the dowsing force. Where samples and colours are introduced these amplify the muscular action by some form of sympathetic resonance somewhere in the harmonic range detected by the brain.

This is reinforced by the mental fixed thought school, which agrees with the above theory in that mental thought or concentration conditions the brain, the nervous computer and controller, to receive only what is required, and neuro-muscular movement occurs in the arms, etc. to overbalance rods over a reaction.

As we know, the body is divided down the middle with reference to the nervous system, the two halves of the brain on opposite sides controlling these independently, except where a common centre plays a controlling part, i.e. the glands, etc. The dowsing force also appears to be detected independently by each side of the body or on either side of the dowsing instrument, hence the direction detection so easily demonstrated by the use of some specialised rods, such as the L rod and the Double V rod (see Figure 1), which will be explained later.

The brain is still being discovered by the medical scientist, and all pointers at present show that our instinctive attributes in conjunction with conscious training bring out many unknown powers we never knew we had, especially when it is connected with the centres controlling self-preservation.

I have noticed in recent articles written by dowsers that advice is frequently given that the various methods used by other dowsers should be ignored and that each one should adhere to his own method if it is appears to work. This to me is not progressive. We can all learn from each other and improve. With proper training we may even discover that there is a common method we really all use in some form or other, and that variations are only to be attributed to differences in our physical make-up. To reinforce this idea, I think it must be agreed that most of us started dowsing by using some well-tried method before we felt the common dowsing force as we know it, and the following

22

known facts will be generally confirmed by all dowsers of experience to exist, but to name a few:—

1. A pull or some form of indication over reactions.
2. The rod position over a reaction.
3. The Bishop's Rule point of reaction.
4. The directional pull or field of a dowsing influence.
5. The effect of samples, actual or colour.
6. Depthing count down.
7. Flow effect.
8. The standing wave effect.
9. Effects due to body polarity.
10. Mental fixed thought in selection.
11. Rod behaviours in their various forms or shapes.
12. Consistent results on repetition.
13. Polarity shift.
14. Fundamental rays and numbers.

I have been particularly impressed in my practical study of different types of dowsing rods to find that definite patterns of behaviour do exist in their behaviour, and if I am right perhaps a concise science could be built up, so as to attract the pure scientist to research with us, to bring us to the notice of the public and thus enable us to lose this " fringe occult " label that many give to our work. The curious fact that the majority of rods all have tips to their physical shape, can this lead to point discharges of electricity and give a pull effect? Or do dowsing rods form a mechanical aid to the neuro-muscular system and help us to detect this dowsing force, which may quite likely be electrical in character?

Listed below are the main types of rods and their characteristics:—

1. *Simple V Rod* This rod, perhaps the best known and most commonly used, is held in both hands in the fingers in such a way that it is held just in balance against collapse of its springy shape in a horizontal plane. This rod may be made of any suitable, pliable, springy material and of a size suitable for handling. A pull upwards or downwards is felt in the rod when over a dowsing reaction. It may be slight, mild or violent. Should the dowser keep a firm grip on the rod and prevent collapse he can feel the force change as he moves over the reaction; he generally terms this the strength of the pull when it is at a maximum. Should one wish to search for a distant object it is necessary with this rod to face in the direction from whence it comes, as one has no sense of pull from either side of the body mid line. This I attribute to the shape of the V rod in that it has only one point and cannot twist either left or right of the body mid line. If held in the vertical plane, however, directional pulls are discernible either side of the body mid line.

The shape of the cross section of this rod widens its qualitities.

23

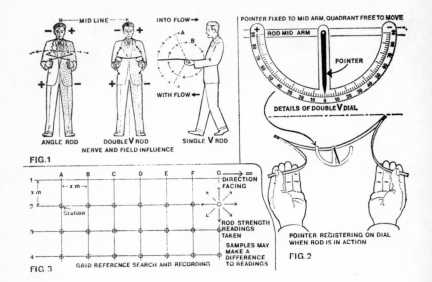

FIG.1

MID LINE — INTO FLOW → POINTER FIXED TO MID ARM, QUADRANT FREE TO MOVE

ROD MID ARM — POINTER

ANGLE ROD — DOUBLE V ROD — SINGLE V ROD

NERVE AND FIELD INFLUENCE

WITH FLOW ←

DETAILS OF DOUBLE V DIAL

POINTER REGISTERING ON DIAL WHEN ROD IS IN ACTION

FIG.2

DIRECTION FACING

Station

ROD STRENGTH READINGS TAKEN

SAMPLES MAY MAKE A DIFFERENCE TO READINGS

FIG 3 GRID REFERENCE SEARCH AND RECORDING

Round rods twist in their lengths, square ones are more rigid and give better skin contact. This skin contact when near the threshold of pain conveys a better sense of rod movement, and this can be useful, although tiring to use. The square ones are useful in detecting force field patterns. Rod sizes vary. Large ones are heavy and tiring to use, but ultra light may be too insensitive. It is therefore best to choose the rod which gives the best results and causes little fatigue when in use. These generally are of reasonable size, say, approximately 1ft. to 1ft. 3ins. long.

2.   *Double V Rod* This rod, now used by a number of people, was accidentally discovered by myself in the spring of 1967 and an article on it was published in the B.S.D. Journal, No. 137 (September 1967).

While making a single V rod out of whalebone one evening, I wondered what would happen if I joined on another arm and created two points. I found it worked in an odd way over a heating pipe which ran under my kitchen floor and was very sensitive. From then on I had to discover what would happen under all the normal conditions. It was a unique opportunity to find out how a rod behaved. Since writing the article on its basic qualities I have made further progress, which will be seen in Figure 4. This new rod, due to its ability to give the direction of the reactions, can be adapted easily to give graduated strength of pull readings by the addition of a pointer fixed to the rod mid bar and gravity operated quadrant marked the full 180°. (See

24

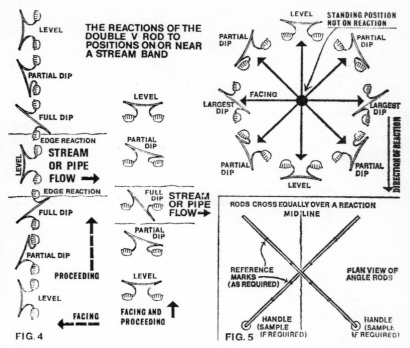

FIG. 4

FIG. 5

THE REACTIONS OF THE DOUBLE V ROD TO POSITIONS ON OR NEAR A STREAM BAND

Figure 2). This graduated double V rod enables the operator to make definite readings as one would on a scientific instrument and so collate the information to form graphs and draw field patterns, which should please the conventional scientist and geologist, etc. With, if necessary, the addition of samples held against the rod, or by recording in notes the mind fixation of your search. All types of reading and recordings are now possible. The readings can be of strengths of reactions direct or of distant influences, and the direction *is* indicated by the readings. (See Figure 3) The rod can be operated at fast walking pace if need be, on uneven ground, in vehicles, trains, etc. The centre arm is unaffected by movement of the body so long as the operator locks his arms in the traditional stance. It is possible to use this rod with the eyes closed, as the rod movements can be felt. This is very useful when auto-suggestion is possibly marring results. The rod is preferably made of flat material such as whalebone or plastic, it is held in the same manner as the traditional rod in the fingers, and rod sensitivity is regulated by pulling the arms apart to the best position. Keep this position now constant if you want consistent readings, (See Figure 2) and allow the rod to settle for at least three seconds for real accuracy before taking readings.

25

3. *The Straight Rod* There are three types of rods found in this shape, and to explain further it is necessary to take each type in turn.

(a) *Held as a wand* The rod is held in the hand at one end as one would hold a sword, the forearm being kept stiff and wrist locked. If the rod is held with the tip over a reaction a sideways motion will develop. This is not easily recognised at first if the reaction is small, so to amplify the movement it is advisable to give a constant gentle up and down whipping movement to the rod; the forces then combine to form a circular motion. (See Figure 6). The full circle means that the dowser is pointing to the reaction. The build-up of the elliptical to circular movement means one is approaching the reaction. This rod will detect distant radiations and is used as one would use a pointer to sight down, preferably keeping it in front of the body mid line. The rod may also be used to dowse vertical surfaces and over one's own head if need be. Samples may be used, with their resulting amplification of movement.

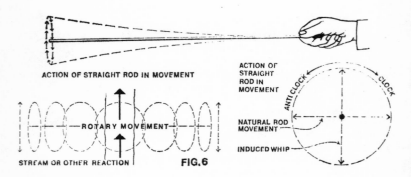

ACTION OF STRAIGHT ROD IN MOVEMENT

ROTARY MOVEMENT

STREAM OR OTHER REACTION

FIG.6

ACTION OF STRAIGHT ROD IN MOVEMENT

ANTI CLOCK

CLOCK

NATURAL ROD MOVEMENT

INDUCED WHIP

(b) *The Balanced Rod.* This is little used. It is finely balanced on the fingers, arm held straight down. It dips or rises to reactions.

(c) *Bow or Curved Rod.* This is held in a similar manner to the Single V rod and reacts in a like manner. A possible recording of this rod in an Assyrian bas-relief (a photograph of which appeared in Journal No. 51, March 1946), shows that this could be one of the earliest forms of rod. This rod is little used nowadays.

4. *Angle Rods.* (See Figures 3 and 5). These rods are widely used and have become quite sophisticated in design. An angle rod is held in each hand and allowed to swing free in the horizontal plane. They are sensitive to reactions in all positions about the

mid body line, and therefore point to the direction from which the reaction is coming, the body being in a single stance position or moving slowly. The disadvantage of this rod is that violent body movement (fast walking over uneven ground, operating in windy conditions) makes recordings difficult or even impossible to indicate. Special markings for reference can be made on the body arms, and it is essential always to keep the hands at a set distance apart if constant readings are required. Most dowsers can operate Angle Rods for simple work. The different rod arm movements experienced in this rod again explain the differential detection of the reactionary influences found on either side of the body mid line. As with other rods, samples held in the handles or hands can help amplify or select results. One grave disadvantage with this rod is that the rod arm positions cannot be felt and it cannot be used with the eyes closed constantly. These rods have been manufactured commercially with some limited success, or can be made from pieces of wire or metal rod.

5. *Motorscopes and Wire Spirals.* These rods have a rotary action on the horizontal plane, the ends being held in the hands in a position as if operating a crank. The Motorscope is a stiff cranked rod or a wire spiral pushed into a cranked shape. When the rods are held over a reaction the hands appear to revolve involuntarily, as if in a muscular spasm. It would be interesting, although I have never tried it, to make a crank which is jointed in the middle, to see if one hand revolves faster or slower than the other. This rod is not used very often, and generally only by the experienced.

From this brief description of the rods and their movements I hope I have given some interest to those who see far more work is necessary to perfect them.

To sum up, I would say that it is now possible to go quite deeply into the patterns of rod movements and recordings of same and to produce some very interesting results from the readings. I am sure the results in many cases will be comparable to those given by orthodox scientific instruments operated by trained specialists from scientific and commercial institutions. I believe properly trained dowsers using graduated rods are able not only to state the feel but to write their findings down on paper (using an assistant) and work out the details at home or office, there being no need to complete the task if carried out over a grid pattern in one operation. A re-visit can be made as needs dictate, as with a scientific recording instrument.

The proper listing and diagramming of information is always more respected by the trained professional, and conclusions can be discussed in more detail, as in laboratory and research work, when examining the findings. The graduated Double V rod method of dowsing used in conjunction with the grid reference (Figure 3) is ideal, i.e. G2/10°C/+60°/B where G2 = station, 10°C =compass direction, +60° = dial reading, B = blue sample.

The human body, after all, is a most remarkable and complex structure containing numerous neuro-muscular mechanisms controlled in some way by the brain, into which many given programmes can be fed. The dowsing sense appears to be instinctive and one of man's protective senses, whether for water-finding, detecting danger, or searching for the essentials of life. Surely it can be used more and more in our daily life for the finding and supplying of our needs. In many commercial fields which need information that they cannot yet find, the rod in the hands of a trained dowser could, I feel, go a long way to supply an answer.

ANGLE RODS
Dr Arthur Bailey

Angle rods are the things that brought me into dowsing, so I have a sort of fellow feeling for them. They were the first things with which I got any dowsing reactions at all. I don't always use angle rods, as I tend to use the weapons that seem best suited to the job. I don't believe in being wedded too firmly to any particular technique. I have discovered through bitter experience that if you learn one particular method you will find sooner or later that you are in no position to use it. I remember talking to Mrs. Fry and she said, " The Bishop's Rule is all right for depthing, but if you are in the position that if you tried to use that method for depthing a stream you would go straight over the cliff of a china clay mine it is a little bit difficult." You therefore have to learn other techniques and this I do quite unashamedly, but angle rods are what I started with and I still use them for some jobs. What I want to do today is tell you about my experiences with angle rods, a little bit of how they work, where they gain over other systems and where they fail.

There is nothing magical about angle rods. Mr. Guttridge, one of our past members, once made a pair of angle rods with gimbal bearings, so that no matter what you did with the handles the rods remained obstinately horizontal, and he defied anyone to use them. I had the opportunity to try the wretched things. I walked along with them and, no matter what I did, the rods pointed straight ahead. They wouldn't do anything, and this confirmed what I had always suspected—that certainly for 99 per cent of dowsers there is no magical force in the angle rods; the " magic " lives within the dowser.

What causes angle rods to move is not the effect of the dowsing field on the metal or what you choose to make the rods out of;

it is the fact that your hands move. You don't know that they are moving and not everybody reacts in the same way. People have done electrical tests to see what goes on. If I take a plain pair of angle rods and go over a stream, all being well the rods will move inwards, because the forearm muscles twist. You may not realise what is happening, but that is what moves the rods.

If you hold a forked rod you will find that if you rotate your arms the forked rod moves, so it is exactly the same driving force. The only snag with the forked rod is that it takes a bit of knack to hold it. I know people who can use neither forked nor angle rods, but if they get something like Thompson's Double V rod it may work for them. The interesting thing about the Double V rod is that if you rotate both your arms nothing at all happens. The Double V rod works on a different mechanism altogether. It works by the hands moving up or down compared with each other, so you are using a different group of muscles.

Now if the dowsing force were directly on the muscles they would react themselves. Well, we know the muscles react, but the interesting thing is that people have coupled dowsers up to electronic instruments and checked to see what goes on and they have found that the muscles get instructions from the brain to change tension, so the reaction is not directly on the muscles. The dowsing reaction comes from a bit further back—from the brain or whatever it is that instructs the brain. What we are doing is pushing the problem further back.

I would like to establish right at the beginning that if we get a muscular reaction it is not necessarily the same for everybody. The instructions from the brain to a certain part of the body to tighten up may differ from one person to another, so if you try angle rods and the forked rod and they don't work do not assume that you cannot dowse. You may be able to get it by tinglings in your fingertips; some people get it by feeling the stomach muscles tense up. People get entirely different reactions. That, I think, is why there has been this mythology in the past that dowsing is for the very few. It is not; the vast majority can dowse. The vast majority may not make very good dowsers; that is a different thing. I would never have made a concert pianist, because I am not, so to speak, built that way. Similarly, I can get reasonable results in dowsing, but I wouldn't claim to be absolutely brilliant.

The problem with the old classical rod is that it takes a lot of holding, as a good deal of force is required to spring it ready to move up or down. If I had to dowse all the afternoon with one of these large rods I should be worn out. When I use a small rod there is no problem, but there is a knack in holding the standard rod, and when I first started dowsing I could do nothing with it. I owe a great debt of gratitude to a French book which I happened to read, which had pictures of bewhiskered dowsers using angle rods. The book recommended handles for angle rods. I discovered that about the best thing for that purpose was ball point pens and two bits of welding rod. With the outside part of the ball-point pens as handles you can hang on as tightly as you wish and it will not affect the swing of the rod, but I must admit I rather like using angle rods bare, so that I can feel the tension build up before they actually move. For a beginner I think is is often easier with handles and it doesn't really matter what they are made of. The main thing is that they should be free to move.

Somebody who carefully checked over my angle rods with a pendulum once said, " You have got the polarity wrong. They are both positive at the end. One should be positive and one should be negative and you should always hold them in the correct hand." I said, " I'm frightfully sorry but they work just the same whichever way I hold them." I think you can go hunting for all sorts of things, and if you believe they help you that's fine. I think ultimately most dowsers finish up with a very simple set of tools, but right at the beginning, if you find yourself in deep water and you can identify something which you think is causing the problem and convince your subconscious mind that that is the cause of the trouble, the odds are that you will then be more successful, although it may not really be that at all. Right at the beginning I think it is very easy, especially for sceptical people like me, to become discouraged. You get a few positive reactions and you find something which you never knew was there. Then all of a sudden doubt sets in, as happens to all of us. You say, " Well, it could have been luck." There is always that little devil inside you busy trying to push you back on to the orthodox strait and narrow, as it were. Really it isn't strait and narrow. It is a great big muddy morass. We like to think that orthodoxy knows all the answers, although it does not.

When I am using a pair of angle rods I just hold them. The movement is due to a muscular twist of the wrist, and if you tip them too far up gravity will come into play and they will just swing towards you. Sometimes people set off and the rods do all sorts of funny things, and they say, " What have I found? " but the odds are that they just haven't learnt the knack of holding them. Personally I always drop the tips down slightly to make sure that gravity does not come into it, and then as you go along and your wrists move the rods move inwards, and the nearer the rods are to horizontal when you start the more sensitive they will become. If you set off with them absolutely horizontal they are in danger of flying round in circles, so if you find your reactions are too strong drop the tips down a bit; then you need a much bigger twist of the wrist to make them move. You don't know you are doing it, and if you try quite deliberately to stop them moving you can do so, but the art of dowsing is to have a neutral mind, an open mind. I can watch myself nearly like another person when I am dowsing, quite interestedly, to see what happens.

Angle rods are very useful, because they can indicate more than a V rod can. If you don't quite know where things are or what you are looking for they can be very helpful in drawing your attention to things, as it were. Suppose I am looking for something which I am fairly certain is in a certain area, if I go walking along with a pair of angle rods they both start pointing to one side. That means there is something worth looking at over there, even if it is not exactly what I am looking for. Once or twice I have found when I was concentrating on a particular thing that they wandered off and pointed to something else, which proved to be extremely important. Angle rods have the great advantage of being able not only to indicate where things are but on which side. With a V rod you cannot really do that. You can modify your performance as you go along to see where you get the maximum reaction from a V rod, but angle rods do it for you, so that as you go along they can point off to one side. You can also tell how strong the reaction is more clearly with angle rods than with the V rod. I get several grades of reaction with the angle rods. If I go over something rather small and insignificant they might move perhaps only an inch or two. If I go over a stream that is hardly worth bothering with, unless somebody is absolutely desperate, they might move in a couple of inches, but when they start meeting and crossing right over, really starting to pull in, you are on to something really worth going for. It isn't just streams you can find—it may be water pipes or any old thing.

A colleague of mine has discovered rather reluctantly that he can dowse—mainly because he saw me doing a job for a friend of his on a local farm. He was surprised by the positive reactions I was getting, in and out, absolutely precise, so he tried it and found that he could do it too. I don't think he is prepared to accept dowsing, but it does work for him very strongly, as he is very sensitive, and he has discovered that he can get absolute accuracy on depth, which he also hadn't expected. The advantage of using things like angle rods is that with a novice they move easily, whereas a V rod doesn't. I gave my colleague a V rod to try and he could get no reaction, because he hadn't learnt the knack of holding it. With the angle rods he was off and away, getting strong and accurate reactions. He is now, I think, wondering whether he dare pursue it very much further.

As a beginner's tool angle rods, I think, are ideal, and as somebody who has been dowsing for a number of years I must admit that I still turn to them quite often, because I find it so easy to get indications of flow rate and things like that right at the beginning. With the V rod I have to go and check things afterwards and I don't

31

get any initial indication as to whether the thing I have found is strong or weak. People probably vary in this.

The problem with angle rods is the wind. If you are using them outdoors and there is a strong wind blowing they will blow all over the place, and that is why I made my super angle rods. These are quite heavy, but their wind resistance is such that I can use them in a reasonably strong wind. They also look rather more scientific, being in heavy metal with ball races in the handles. If I am going out on a posh job somewhere I always shine them up. They look all the better for it and it often helps. Again it depends on what you are doing. If you are working in an area where people are scientifically minded they are a bit more likely to believe in something that looks semi-scientific than in an old piece of wood. The fact is, of course, that you can get equally adequate results with either. These angle rods have ball races, so they swing exceedingly easily, but a lot of people pick them up and cannot get anything sensible out of them *because* they are so free-moving. You can, in fact, get a bit of friction on these rods by tightening a screw down on to the shaft inside, so that they don't swing so easily, but normally I leave them perfectly free. These rods took a lot of making; there are ball races top and bottom and it took a fair bit of engineering to sort them out.

Then I went on to the Mark 2 version, which was going back towards the simple version. They are just made out of plastic " Tufnol," a single ball bearing at the top and plain sleeve bearing at the bottom. This attaches them just as easily and they are much easier to make. They are the ones I usually take with me. The rods screw out and you can store them in a small space. The fact that the handle is insulated doesn't make any difference. Some people say, " Surely the handle shouldn't be metal? " or, in this case, " Surely the rods shouldn't be metal? " You can forget it. The people who say you have got it all wrong are like the person who saw my metal pendulum and winced and said, " It should be made out of natural things. The bob should be hazelwood and the thread should be cotton." I produced my beechwood pendulum and she brightened up but asked, "What is the thread? " I replied " Nylon," and she said, " Oh dear! " It matters not, so far as I know. If you think it matters then it matters; it is as simple as that, but ultimately I use whatever comes to hand.

I think you can easily brainwash yourself into believing certain things are necessary when they are not necessary at all. If you study the history of dowsing, particularly if you look back through the Journals, you will see how complicated people made it originally and how over the years it has been simplified. At the beginning there was this mythology that one should look for bigger and better pendulums with magnets in them and all sorts of things.

32

I don't decry magnets. I know some people use pendulums with magnets in them and get exceptional results. But to a beginner I would say that, so far as I am aware, it makes no great difference what you use. Ultimately it is the person behind it that matters.

Now these are just simple angle rods. They have no calibration on them, and if you like you can deck out your angle rods until they look like Christmas trees. In fact, there is one gentleman who produces beautiful angle rods, chromium-plated, with markers all over them and a receptacle to put a sample in. All I can say is that I don't need them, but again it is a big problem to know what is necessary. You can make them with little adjustable slides or put washers on. There was a Revealer which was made by a Leeds firm—I don't think it is still being made—and used to cost about £60. Basically it had angle rods of the type with ball races. It also contained some metallic filings inside, which apparently were intended to produce a magical result; a set of samples which you could pull towards you, and calibration bits down the rods.

So far as I am concerned I can get a good idea of how strong the stream is by the way the rods move. If they cross right in and I can really feel a twist on my arms I know there is a thundering big underground flow. If I wanted to know how much was there I shouldn't dream of using little bits of washers glued on the rods. I should use the count down method, or, if there was a stream here, just walk over it. If the rods moved a small amount it would mean 1,000 gallons per hour. If there were 2,000 gallons they would move in further. You can narrow it down further by watching the reactions. Accuracy on flow depends upon the person, but if you get within 20 per cent or 30 per cent you are doing well.

Incidentally, on flow rates I don't think you can do better than follow the practice of one of our Vice-Presidents, Mr. Bill Youngs, who always works out what flow he thinks it is and then divides it by something like factor 2. He does the same with depth, i.e. if he thinks the stream is at 100ft. he will always say 102 or 103ft. He says if they get to the water early they always pull his leg and say, " You were wrong," but it gives a margin for error. And when they test bore and find they have more volume than they expected they say, " Ah, you were wrong. We got more than that. " He says, " That's fine. I don't mind. But if you are 2ft. out on the wrong side they don't half go for you. Equally if you say 10,000 gallons per hour and they only get 9,000 they tend to criticise." Therefore he always prefers to be on the pessimistic side, so if all is well and they find water any difference will always be on their side. He knows he is a bit out, but at least it gives a margin for the unexplained things that can trip anybody up.

What tripped me up right at the beginning was reading books about the Bishop's Rule, which said that you put a mark on the centre of the stream. The method used by Major Creyke was to insert an iron rod, or preferably a numetal rod. I have never forgotten going to my first Congress and seeing Clive Thompson walk out with a large iron crowbar for depthing. It was a sight to behold. Of course, it worked perfectly well, but so far as I know it matters not if you rely on numetal or anything else. If *you* think it is necessary it *is* necessary. If you think you have got to walk out at right angles it is necessary, but I find I get just the same answer whether I walk out at right angles to the stream or in any other direction.

What I found earlier on that was odd was that I got a reaction—I can now manage to shut it out—at half the depth as well as at the full depth. Now Bill Youngs does this, in fact, he walks out until he gets a reaction, then walks back across the stream until he gets another reaction on the other side, and the two distances together are equal to the depth. In other words, he gets a big reaction at half the depth of the stream, measured horizontally from the centre. The fact that I got a reaction at half the distance explains how I came to dig down 10ft. for a stream that was 20ft. down. It was my first experiment and I am glad that it was my stream, not somebody else's. We are getting a bit nearer to it now. I think the neighbours thought it was a peculiar sort of activity, but this summer they have been rather more sympathetic. Certainly we are now getting water out of it, although we are not yet right on the stream, purely because digging down a 14ft. hole is not easy and takes time.

So you can find the depth by all sorts of methods. If you find a stream and you don't know what the depth is, as I said earlier, you might on occasion have to walk over the edge of the cliff if you tried to ascertain the depth by Bishop's Rule or something like that, but you could just walk backwards and forwards, saying, " Is it less than 50ft. down? Is it 10ft., 20ft., 30ft., etc.? " That is the way I tend to work with angle rods and it is much easier than using the V rod. You see it gradually creeping up on you, and when it hits the maximum what I would do would be to check very carefully in 1ft. increments and mentally reject anything that is 2ft. away, so that you get a very positive reaction at the exact figure and reject everything else. It is a relaxation method of mathematics. You get to within 10ft. either side of it, then narrow it down to 5ft. either side, then 2ft., until finally you have got it. That is the method I use for depthing where I cannot pace it out.

If you are using Bishop's Rule, or whatever you like to call it, where you pace it out, the one thing you should always take with you is measuring tape. My pace used to be a yard. I think I must have grown a bit or my legs have grown longer, because it is now nearly a metre when I am deliberately pacing, so I have to be careful. I nearly made a mess of it recently for somebody purely on this account. The difference between a yard and a metre is only 10 per cent and 10 per cent of a foot isn't much, but on 20ft. it is 2ft. If you say they are going to find water at 20ft. and they dig down 20ft., perhaps through good, solid rock, and find nothing, it costs quite a lot to go down another 2ft. So always carry a measuring tape; it looks more professional, too.

If in doubt check by another method to make sure that you are right. If I get a good strong reaction I am happy; I know I am all right. It is the slightly doubtful reactions that I worry about, when one gets the feeling that there is something not quite right. The best thing to do in a case like that is to go away and think about it and then come back, or try another method, or just sit down and do nothing for twenty minutes, or go for a short walk just to clear your mind. There is no point in pushing anything in dowsing; that is when you make mistakes. If somebody has asked you to do a job and when you wake up in the morning you don't feel up to it and everything feels wrong, just ring up and make some plausible excuse to put him off until you feel up to it, rather than sail in and make a hash of it. It always depends on what is involved. Sometimes there is a mad panic and you feel you have just got to do something, but usually that is the one to be careful of, unless it does not involve much expense. If somebody is going to sink a 2,000ft. borehole he is not usually worried about an odd day, because it is going to take quite a long time to sink the borehole. The more money involved, the more careful you have to be that you are on top of the job; it is as simple as that. If you are a beginner it is best to start off with nice easy things and gradually work your way up, but sooner or later somebody will come along with a job rather bigger than you expect. The main thing is to sail into it with the same degree of confidence as with other jobs, but if you feel unhappy about it, if you are not getting the right sort of reactions and feel that you cannot do the job, be careful!

I haven't so far mentioned samples. People say, " How do you know it is a stream? How do you know it isn't a rock fault? How do you know that the stream is there now, that it isn't remanence? " I think this is always a problem. An eager beginner takes a pair of rods, goes along and gets reactions and says, " Marvellous! It works! What have I found? " That is where all the trouble starts. On archaeological sites, which I have worked on, this is the ten thousand dollar question, because those sites are littered with all sorts of bits and pieces. I have worked on maps of archaeological sites and I do use crosses to mark reactions, but normally I do not expect those crosses to form patterns. I use them to indicate anomalies, something there which has yet to be discovered, but I couldn't agree more with Enid

35

about what to do when looking for water. Don't put in a series of crosses and join them up, or you might get it all wrong. If you are working on the map of an archaeological site and if you get a series of crosses that seem to form a straight line, the best thing is to check along that line. I do it with angle rods with somebody else moving a pencil along. I watch my angle rods and if they remain steady it is a straight line feature. If they go in and out, whatever I have got is either a series of separate objects or perhaps a series of diagonally crossing lines.

To find out what you have located is often the most difficult part. I started off by using samples, and then I read about some experiments where somebody had given dowsers separate samples but, unbeknown to the dowsers, had changed the materials within the samples. It was found that if the dowser thought the sample was copper he would react as if it was copper, even if in fact it was aluminium. This rang a little bell with me in the sense that so long as you are conversant with the material there is no need for a sample. If you are not conversant with it a sample may be a useful prop. Usually I don't think it is useful, but if one is asked to look for some very odd thing and a mental prop is needed, a sample is what I would prefer. I have, however, looked for land drains with samples and have been no more successful with samples than without them. In the case I have in mind the nature of the ground in which the drains were placed was far more important than the carrying of samples. I could find land drains on one side of a wall, where there was good, deep topsoil about 2 feet down, but not on the other side, where the topsoil was very thin and there was solid clay underneath. I tried samples on both sides of the wall and certainly I found the drains on one side but not on the other. I think the difference in the ground was responsible, although I am not absolutely certain why. They were finally located, but the results I was getting, although better than chance, were nothing like spot on, which I would normally have expected to be on something like that.

Samples can help but you have to be careful not to override them. I have told this tale before, but it is worth telling again. A dowser came to our house with a beautiful set of rods with rotating samples. You could set a sample of whatever you wanted—coal, oil, water, etc. To illustrate it he said: " I will set it to something very unusual. I won't tell you what I have set it to." He went into the house and walked along and off swung the angle rods to one side, and he said, " There you are. I've set it to mercury and it's reacting to your barometer." Well, I hadn't the heart to tell him that it was an aneroid barometer with an alcohol thermometer, with not an atom of mercury in it. If the dowsing rods had worked properly they would have swung off to the other side, where I had a clinical thermometer in the bathroom.

Now if I had been a sceptic on dowsing I should have said immediately, " That finishes it. It's a load of rubbish." But the point is that he had picked up our barometer before he could see it and he evidently had a picture in his own mind of a barometer, because he said, " There you are." He hadn't been looking for mercury, he had been looking for a barometer, telling himself that it must contain mercury, as all old-type barometers did, so his dowsing was accurate. The samples had nothing to do with it, as he had overridden them. It was what was living in his mind that mattered.

I still tend to use the Mager rosette. If I find water a quick run round the rosette with just one angle rod is a very quick way of finding out the quality. If I get a reaction on purple or blue I am happy; it is drinkable. The nearer I am to purple the happier I am, but I find that blue is tap water quality, although nothing like as good as purple. If I get a reaction further round I know that it will be mineralised to a fair degree and I have to go and check which mineral it is—calcium, iron, magnesium—to find the concentration and whether it is going to cause any trouble. Grey means either lead or pollution. Either way it is not the sort of water you would want for yourself or for watering stock. If it is black I wouldn't touch it with a barge pole. So I accept the Mager rosette as a useful prop. If I get a reaction round past blue I know it is worthwhile checking to see if there are any problems, but if it is in the blue/purple I know there won't be any problems. It is an easy method of getting a rapid answer, but if I happen not to have put it into my pocket I don't worry. It has its uses but I can do without it.

I have talked to quite a number of experienced dowsers and they say samples are a useful prop to start off with but they tend to do without them later. So long as you find they help you it is all right to use them. If like Clive Thompson you put a sample at the end of your rod, so that you just react to one thing, that is fine. All I can say is that I personally can get on as well without them. I will admit that when I started dowsing it wasn't all that easy to get a mental picture of what I was looking for. If you accept samples at the beginning as a useful prop to be put down at some later date that is fine.

Now I am going to do a bit of free advertising. I don't get anything for it. There is a book on dowsing called " Dowsing: Techniques and Applications " writted by Tom Graves, who is one of our members. It is the best exposition of dowsing that I have come across. He works on the basis that to do it you have got to try it out. He doesn't theorise much, he gives all the basic methods and says, " This is the way that people do it. Now try it." He doesn't make it complicated, as it is in some of the BSD Journal articles and particularly in " Practical Dowsing Symposium." I remember reading an article in the Symposium about water flows, with all sorts of reflected zones, etc., and I thought, " I shall never find water with all this lot." I can only say, thank goodness I don't pick any of these things up, and I dare say a lot of them only exist if you think they do. If you don't think they exist you won't find them, but I would give a warning: if you have two streams at the same depth coming towards each other, beware! If they are flowing out of the same rock stratum it is possible to find a strong line of reaction halfway between the two. I was able to explain to a publican why no water had been found when he had sunk quite a deep well on the advice of someone who had discovered he could dowse. There were two streams which came very close together and then, in fact, broke out of the hillside a little lower down. The dowser knew one of them came out but he hadn't spotted the other, and the line which he had picked up was the dividing line between then. They were both nearly equal in strength, so he had carefully gone to the best place on the centre line, where a big hole had been sunk. The publican was very worried because the " stream " line which had been followed had only just gone into his property and out again, whereas there was a perfectly good stream (one of the two mentioned) running past his back door, a much better place. He asked should he dynamite it further down. I said, " Heavens! Wherever there's water don't use dynamite or you will very likely lose it." In this case the water flows in the bedding plane in nearly horizontal strata.

But to return to the problem of identifying the halfway point between two streams, I once nearly fell into the trap myself. I don't say I always react that way, but it is always well worth checking to see if there is more than one stream going in the same direction to make sure that you have not picked up anything odd. Some people do pick up side reactions from the stream. Thank goodness I never have done.

I don't think there is an easy way forward once you have picked up the rudiments of dowsing. The difficulty can be finding the way in and that is where Tom Graves' book is so useful, but once you have got started the main thing is it's up to you!

THE ROLE OF THE SAMPLE IN DOWSING
Abbe Mermet

(*Translated from the French by R. J. Mackay*)

I thank you, Mr. President, for the honour you have paid me by inviting my opinion on the part played in Dowsing by what is conventionally called the sample (*témoin*). The following are the views on this question of a dowser of nearly fifty years' experience.

Firstly, it seems to be a fact of experience that when a sub-stance is placed in the vicinity of another substance of the same nature, up to a certain distance which diminishes with the mass, in such manner as I may illustrate by saying that the maximum distance is of the order of 50cm. for weights of about 200gr., and of an order of 30cm. for weights of about 20gr., there is set up between these two bodies what seems to be a " line of sympathy " which is detectable by my pendulum and, if I hold the latter half-way between the two bodies, it goes into oscillation in a straight line between these two bodies.

I regard this phenomenon as constituting a " law of likes." It is on this fact which rests, for me, the possibility of utilizing the " sample." If, in effect, instead of placing the two bodies on the same horizontal plane, I put one of them, or merely a fragment of one of them, in the hand with which I hold my pendulum, I find that the latter swings in a straight line towards the neighbouring body, which *seems* to attract it after the manner of a magnet. In my prospecting, therefore, if I am looking for copper, I take care to hold a sample of copper in my hand ; if I am looking for water, I hold in my hand a tube containing water, or a wet rag, and similarly, for every other substance, I carry in my hand a body of the same nature.

But in which hand should the sample be held ? Is it a matter of indifference whether it is placed in the hand which holds the pendulum, or in the other hand ? My unhesitating answer is the following : The pendulum and the sample should be held in one and the same hand. It is for me a fact of experience, the reason for which seems to me to be that the pendulum, having as its objective the detection of a body's radiation, and the sample that of reinforcing this radiation, it appears logical that pendulum and sample should be held by the same hand, so as to obtain the maximum of direct and the minimum of parasitic action.

But, some will ask, is it not a fact that many experimentalists hold their samples in the opposite hand from the one which holds the pendulum, and get results ? My answer is as follows : If they obtain good results, it is a case of one or other of two things : either, unconsciously, they are sensitive to the effects of a sort of " mental radiation " which is capable of acting in all direc-tions, or else that they hold the " sample " hand so far from their body that the sample may be no more than an element in a phenomenon of similitude, which must be treated as if the sub-stance in question were on the ground, or on a piece of furniture.

I therefore maintain as a certainty that the sample thus placed in the opposite hand to the one which holds the pendulum has, *by itself*, no value, and has no more effect upon the sensitivity of the operator than would be so if his hand were empty.

Let us now examine what, in a general way, is the importance of the sample, considered by itself. In my opinion it is effective in three ways :—

(i.) It *reveals*, in a given neighbourhood, the presence of a substance identical with that of which the prospector has a fragment in his hand.

(ii.) It *reinforces* the potential of receptivity in regard to the substance to be detected.

(iii.) Finally, it renders possible the making of certain *qualitative analyses*.

Thus, for example, let us suppose that my detector has revealed to me the presence of a seam of coal. But what kind of coal ? To find out, I will place in my hand, in turn (in my pendulum hand), samples of very volatile coal, medium household, and anthracite ; and if the pendulum, for example, gives a normal reaction with the medium household sample only, I shall know that the pendulum comes to rest before medium household coal.

For myself, a sample is indispensable for making a *qualitative* analysis in connection with mineral prospection.

I consider, on the other hand, that for the detection of a hidden body, a sample can most often play only a secondary role. Thus I find the sample effective only on condition that it will be the only factor in operation, which is very rare, and when the mental factor is totally withdrawn. It is the mental factor, then, which plays the main part, whether we are aware of it or not. The effect of the mental factor is much more powerful than that of the sample, to such an extent that the latter is completely overwhelmed by the former when they act together. A simple experiment shows this.

Have a sample of coal in your hand and think only of your coal : if a seam exists in the neighbourhood, the pendulum will react over the coal, and you will be able to pass over a current of water without becoming aware of it. But if, with your coal sample still in your hand, you lose sight at a given moment of your quest for coal, to think about the possibility of the existence of subterranean water, in search of which your mind suddenly veers, you would then be able to pass over a rich carboniferous seam without feeling it ; everything happens as if the cerebral act in question had stifled the physical phenomenon which was previously established between the coal sample and the coal seam.

In practice, then, without discussing here either the nature or the mode of action of the mental factor, my conclusion will be that you must obey the proverb " *Age quod agis* "—Do what you are doing. You must think of what you wish to find, and of nothing but that. On this condition only can the " sample " bring effective help which, as I have indicated above, can sometimes go so far as to render impossible a complete qualitative analysis.

COLOUR IN DOWSING

Clive Thompson

Among the many subjects of study and usage in the art of dowsing that still require to be fully explained is that of colour. Whether we realise it or not, colour has a great effect on our lives both mentally and physically, for without it our world would indeed be very dull and uninteresting.

In the art of dowsing it has long been known that if a dowser holds or places a sample of the material against or on the dowsing instrument he uses, the effect is to amplify his dowsing sense in the detection of that material and it tends to cut out all stimulations of other materials. This sample of material is in the dowser's language called " a witness." Soon after the turn of this century those who researched our subject found that the use of colours had this " witness " effect and they started their own studies and methods to find out what happened. One only has to read in our library books about the work done by Mager and others to find this out. To date no satisfactory explanation has been offered other than that there appears to be a link between the natural vibration of matter and colours. Colours, in fact, may work on a harmonic scale, the reaction being noted when a form of resonance takes place which can be detected by the dowser, a theory I strongly support up to the present. Maybe the researches in microvibratory physics will one day be able to confirm this?

The most easily read book on the subject of colour in dowsing and how to experiment with it was written by Captain W. H. Trinder and entitled " Dowsing." In it he explains the use of the rosette developed by Mager, a French engineer. The rosette has eight basic colours in this order: Violet, blue, green, yellow, red, grey, black and white. Violet is placed on the colour circle in the position North and the remainder take their positions in a clockwise direction. The colours appear to have an affinity with the cardinal points, red being South.

You will note that in the Mager rosette the primary colours red, yellow and blue are present, together with the secondary colours green and violet, plus grey, black and white, the last three being the two extremes and their mixture and reflective value. The rosette is thus unique in its choice of colour order.

The Mager rosette has been found by most users of colours in dowsing to be a very handy reference instrument to study and carry out their work. Orange, the missing secondary colour, is found to be in its naturally expected place lying between yellow and red. When the selection of the innumerable colour hues is required these can be located adjacent to their parent colours with reference to the Mager colour order. The study of this subject is so vast that I have so far not tried all colours against the rosette

41

colour order, and I must admit there may be some rogue colours of a particular hue which do not follow the pattern when used for dowsing purposes.

For those dowsers who use true physical samples or witnesses to touch or hold or place on their dowsing instruments while working the great disadvantage has always been purity, or difficulty in physical size, or even their being unobtainable when required. Rods and pendulums have been made with special receptacles for the samples or witnesses, some very elaborate and complicated, but always there has been a limit to the amount a dowser can carry, especially when away on some distant site, where samples are not easy to find. The fact that colour in all its hues has been found by dowsers to have an affinity with, and a sensitivity to, physical materials shows where colours have their advantage. One may carry a Mager rosette or vast collection of colour samples in a small space when out on a survey; the choice can be very great in number. After finding out the colour reference of a physical material the colour can be used as the witness, or conversely a colour may be used as a witness and the physical material discovered identified either " on site " or at one's leisure " off site." The fact that one can obtain a colour reaction and reference on site is most interesting, because if this is obtained and noted the dowser who does not know what the true reference is can possibly identify the material later, this being found from the operator's own material-colour schedule or coding system reference, and later work immediately eliminates the possibility of precognition, guesswork or sheer trickery, all points being those the sceptic looks for and what the dowser least wants to affect the accuracy of his work.

In identifying materials and coding their colours I follow generally the method explained by Trinder in his book, i.e. I hold a black pendulum or rod over the various individual colours on the Mager rosette while holding a sample, and note how the pendulum or rod behaves over each colour. The reactions will vary in strength or may not move at all. Make a note of the behaviour of the rod or pendulum, especially with the colour that gives the greatest reaction. You will then have a code of the colour sympathy or reaction to the material. The code you may prefer to use is the strongest reaction to a particular colour, or you may use the whole colour reference relating to the rosette, for example— very strong on red, small on white, nil on the rest, and so on. I find that I generally only note the strongest reaction and use that, but use the other further references only when I have near coincidences of reference. Note, however, that these secondary reactions may not be very reliable. Further lists can usually be made by using the joint colours on the rosette or the mixture of two or more colours. Further hues may be selected from separate colour samples. The choice is thus endless. The sound result must and should be repeatable.

I mentioned the use of the pendulum because it is generally handy, but the same test can be applied by using rods and checking the strength of the reaction. The Double V rod which I developed, combined with its gravity operated quadrant strength gauge, is ideal, using one point only over the colour or sample, as a strength figure can be read from the gauge, which can be noted in numerical form. I recommend black for the operating instrument, as most are made in black material, and the tests will then be carried out with black as a constant to be combined with selected colours as required.

My further experiments with colour are an improvement on the method just mentioned. I have found that if the fingers only contact a selected colour, or if the instrument is made in the selected colour, results are far more positive and trustworthy. For this purpose I have developed a system whereby sleeves in selected colours are placed on the handled ends of pendulum strings and rods. The effect of the reaction is limited to the colour of the sleeve. It is most important that the fingers must only touch the colour. The effect of handling coloured material possibly filters the effect of reactions which are received by the operator, rod or pendulum. It appears to me that the body in the form of the hands and fingers and the rod held together become a combined instrument in detecting dowsing forces. Colours thus become the tuning agents in the detection of the highest resonance of the microvibratory-physical field in the individual test of selecting materials by the use of sympathetic colours, assuming all matter is in constant vibration on its own microvibrationary frequency.

The subject and use of colour in practical dowsing becomes more and more interesting as you use it in dowsing searches. When a colour is used as a substitute witness to the true physical witness it is very accurate and useful. For example, I have found that red is sympathetic to iron, green to copper, green to oil (here shades and hues need to be further examined for maximum strength and identification, etc.), orange to gold, violet to pure water and silver, grey to lead, blue to electricity and mildly tainted water, grey to reasonably foul water, black to sewage and putrid matter, coal and phenol, white to voids, to mention a few.

The above colour references to materials may not be the same for everyone, because each dowser must find his own colour references by making his own individual tests. This is not surprising, as every individual differs from every other and appears to vibrate at a different rate. All the dowsing methods I have tried and tested out on others when multi-selective dowsing methods have been attempted have shown that colour gives the most consistency and near universal results.

I have found that dowsing reactions detected by the standard black rods and pendulums cannot always be felt. However, when they are colour treated they show reactions. When they show a nil reaction that must be the colour acting as a shield or filter. When a hue shield colour in the form of a sheet of material in the filter colour is placed over the dowsing reaction the rod should cut out and no reaction be felt. Here possibly is a use for colours in the medical field in order that harmful radiations can be reduced or cut off!

In my investigations I have found that radium in the form of pitchblende sends out violent reactions on all the Mager colours except yellow, when no reaction is felt. Possibly here is a field of research that could be investigated further.

I know of one person, if my memory serves me well, who found success in keeping her wristwatch going by applying a red coloured backing to the watch. Before that it refused to go properly and it was always stopping. I think the red colour acted as a filter in this case.

Fully coloured rods, pendulums, wands, etc. may be used in all the various colours and it is possible to build up quite a collection. These are especially useful when you want to find a selected and coded article. I generally use colourless pendulum strings if the pendulum is self-coloured. Nylon fishing line is ideal for this purpose.

Some operators of rods both past and present have applied coloured ends to their dowsing instruments or applied different systems of colour selection on the stems of stick-like pendulums. Testing and working with all types of instruments is the only way to find which work the best. The stick pendulum with its collar selector that can be moved over various colours may, I suspect, be influenced by its varying gravitational pull due to the different weight distribution caused by moving the collar. Tests must contain no difference in physical weight position or the result is suspect. The length of the pendulum string should be constant while colour testing for the same reason, otherwise selection is being made by adjustment of the pendulum's own natural swinging time.

Those who have studied colour and tried a colour test over another person as well as themselves will soon have discovered that everyone has a personal colour which is strongest. He or she may have secondary colours of varying strengths and even some colours which will not react over them. Use the Mager rosette colour range for easy reference. In good health a person's colour remains constant. In sickness some say it changes and thus a diagnosis can be made of that illness. The basic colour test could be tried over affected parts of the body and notes taken of the result. Abnormal colour radiations may be detected and give warning of trouble. I leave the rest to those who are medically trained. Let them make their research into this subject.

I do not know of a field of dowsing research which would not benefit from a study of colour. For example, buried bones from an archaeological site which I surveyed reacted to yellow when tested. On another occasion a yellow emitting area was detected behind a protective earth barrier on a particular building site which I was called to examine. I was puzzled but concluded that there was quite likely a deposit of bones in the earth. When later the area was examined human bones were found, obviously those of a burial.

Roman pottery emits green, so when searching a Roman site I use green sleeves on my rod to find the pottery.

On sites where you are asked to find one, two or more specific items take your best colour references and use them. But it is when you are asked what is under the site with no reference to anything known to be there that the colour method comes into its own. All sites have a colour pattern. Find out this colour pattern by plotting and testing against your known colour reactions or against samples found on site.

I have recently been on one site trying to locate two capped off mine shafts under 50ft. of spoil overfill badly contaminated with chemical waste. I plotted where I think these are and they are to drill and see if my location is correct.

On another site the pile foundations were altered due to an aquifer being present. I detected this with violet blue and depthed it. They tested my report, found the watercourse and replotted the piles in the area affected, because piles must be bored in a dry subsoil to be effective.

In another instance a live electric main laid in the subsoil needed to be located. Using blue, which to me reacts to live electricity, I located the cable easily and plotted it—far faster, in fact, than the electricity engineer with his electric induction detector. This engineer incidentally left the site saying it was a waste of his time being there when the dowser could detect and locate the main more quickly. The results were correct on examination when they ultimately dug for the cable.

A subsoil laid telephone cable was found by me, using a rod and green leaves from a tree as my colour sample, when I had no other ready-made sample with me. Copper to me is green. Thus I was finding the copper wire.

I always first attempt to find drains by using white as the sample. It reacts to voids, which is more consistent with drains, as they very rarely run full but are generally in a semi-dry state with a small run of foul water in them. If in doubt, test for foul water by all means. Manhole covers are made of iron. Red reacts to iron, so follow the drain until you find a red reaction and a junction of pipes, then you will be able to find lost manholes when required.

Violet is the purest of water fit to drink. Look for the violet reaction of an aquifer when water finding. Should it only be required for animals blue will do, but avoid other colours, especially grey or black. The metal lead is detected by grey, so water tainted by grey could easily have lead in it.

Don't forget that colour works in all directions. The Double V rod can indicate reactions very easily from a great distance, in fact, it behaves like a radio detector with its gravity gauge to measure its fine tuning on direction and pull. Be warned, however, for in one instance I was in a deep basement dig for a new office block and I thought I was detecting iron (red) under my feet, only to find on looking above my head that I was standing under a steel scaffolding tower.

When recently asked to find brine well heads which were inadequately capped off in waste ground under overfill I tested for brine and found that it was sympathetic to green. I located two of the wells by this method, but it was not easy, because the pipes were only 8in. diameter. I got confirmation by using red colour sleeves, which detected the iron lining pipes.

I would stress again that before going too deeply into colour you must please remember that the colours which you find work for you are the ones you should follow. If any colour should differ from someone else's colour reference don't worry, we are not all made alike. It is the results that count, coupled with hard work, commonsense and, may I say, some general knowledge (specialised being all the more reliable) of the subject you are examining, be it water finding, geology, archaeology, medicine, architectural site work, civil engineering, well boring, etc., etc. Treat the use of colour as an amplifier to your senses, for that is what appears to happen, so that your natural range may be extended and your dowsing capabilities greatly widened.

One warning: Do not expect a constant repeat test, as in laboratory tests. The first test is always the most accurate and reliable in the case of dowsing. The mind, body or whatever controls our dowsing senses is too sensitive for " parlour trick " dowsing. Genuine dowsing site jobs prevent the mind worrying if you are getting the proper reaction. Let all reactions occur naturally without undue pressure from other persons around. Sceptics have a common attitude to all unknown sciences. It is a natural reaction in the case of those who orbit in a narrow trained study requiring recurrent, repeatable results. The mind and body with its delicate senses is a very sensitive instrument, far more sensitive than most of the man-made detecting instruments. As

46

time progresses more is being revealed by medical research in proving this is so. Dowsing results are well above a chance ratio, and case histories prove that dowsing is one of man's senses, possibly his sixth natural sense.

PROXY DOWSING

Clive Thompson

I have called this lecture "Proxy Dowsing," firstly because the title is short and easy to remember and secondly because it can be defined as "that of operating dowsing techniques using another person or agent to do the walking over the site of the search." One is always being faced with the problem of explanation and of finding recognisable terms in order to describe our art and its operation. I hope this definition meets with general approval.

I have found after much experimentation that I can apply dowsing techniques to find out site information using another person who is either engaged in dowsing by himself or not actually in the act. In both cases they can be aware or not that you are using them and receiving their reactions from the ground upon which they stand. These persons may be within your sight or out of your sight; it does not seem to matter. Complications only start to occur when the distance between the proxy dowser and yourself is such that you cannot easily communicate with him by word of mouth and it becomes necessary to resort to mechanical signal aids such as sound, visual or electronic means, i.e. walkie-talkie, etc. Visual connection is obviously helpful in order to see one another, but if this is impossible an assistant who is in sight of both yourself and the proxy will be needed in order to do any plotting of reactions when indicated. To sum up, you yourself do not have to be over the site to find reactions; just send someone else and follow him wherever he goes and you will receive the reactions he is experiencing, whether he is aware of them or not. However, you must have some good method to plot his position as necessary.

When using this form of dowsing it is quite obvious that it is done without much effort on your part. You can remain on a location of your own choice and in comfort if you so desire, for it is the proxy dowser who has to do the walking, climbing, clambering over the site and other tedious operations in the search.

If you are on an actual dowsing operation and wish to use a "proxy" but have been unable to get the voluntary assistance of another person, all you have to do is select someone you see in the vicinity to make a search, form your dowsing contact with him in your mind and follow him. It is not essential that the "proxy" knows you are doing this, the only difficulty in this case being that you won't be able to contact him verbally or by signal if you do not wish him to know what you are doing. You will therefore have to follow him visually and do your best to plot by sight when he is standing over a reaction that you are receiving from him. However, with experience I am sure that all who try this method of dowsing will work out their own solutions to the problem.

So far, you may say, proxy dowsing seems a bit far-fetched, but believe me it does work, much to *my* amazement. It is, in fact, so simple that it can turn you into a lazy dowser in that you make others do all the foot slogging on sites. Why not try it, for so many sites are very dirty and hard work to survey by foot.

My first introduction to this form of dowsing was by reading a section of a dowsing book, which very briefly mentioned that it was experienced by a French priest. Being broad-minded, an essential when dealing with all dowsing subjects, I was determined to have a try and behold! it worked. After that I was on my own to try all manner of methods of the dowser's skills to see which would work with "proxy dowsing,"—researching and perfecting experiments in the process. So far I seem only to have just touched the subject, and I am sure there is a long way to go before it will be fully exhausted.

All forms and methods of dowsing techniques may be tried, using rods and pendulums. I use by preference the double V rod which I discovered and developed, and the straight wand. Both are admirable rods for this sort of dowsing, the most accurate I find being the double V itself.

To explain the type of reaction one receives from the proxy dowser I will refer to the double V rod, which I hold in the standard position, always allowing incidentally at least a ten second period for the rod to settle down before starting any operating search. I then instruct the proxy dowser to walk slowly over the site, and I fix in my own mind that I am to follow him and feel any reaction which I choose, that he may pass over. I often use with my rod a sample aid, such as a true sample or preferably a colour sample. When the proxy dowser approaches a dowsing reaction the left hand point of the double V will start to slowly move down to a low position and will be followed by the right hand point, which will move also to a low position. Then suddenly the whole rod will flick upwards, or if held firmly will remain exactly in line. I find this is the indication that the proxy dowser is over the reaction. Should he then proceed over the reaction and carry on walking, one point of the double V will commence to lift up slowly, followed by the other point, to level off eventually at the high position. Every dowser who tries this form of dowsing technique will have to ascertain by practice the true rod position, whatever type is used, to indicate a reaction.

With regard to the straight rod I hold this in a downward position at an approximate angle of 45°, holding it with a stiff forearm and gripping it as if holding a sword, giving it a gentle up and down whipping movement. As the proxy dowser approaches the reaction the rod will start to make an oval indication at its end, and when the proxy is over the reaction the movement will develop into a pure circular shape. As the proxy walks away from the reaction the rod end movement will return to the oval shape and eventually to the up and down movement. Depth bands, when you want them, are indicated by minor movements similar to those experienced over major reactions. Such is the pattern of the straight rod.

If you wish to test yourself with this form of dowsing I advise you to seek the co-operation of a competent fellow-dowser and use him as a proxy, with him ascertaining your accuracy in locating dowsing reactions. When practising try to screen yourself or turn your back to the proxy dowser and see if your accuracy is good. In this case vocal signals between the two of you will generally have to be resorted to; practice makes perfect.

Follow the guide lines I have already given when carrying out this experiment by selecting someone who is unaware of your wish to use him as a proxy, and seeing if your reactions coincide with his reactions on the site over which he is walking.

Dowsers and other interested parties are always trying to find out how the art works. It still baffles the scientific world and even the expert practising dowser, but do not be dismayed; if it works, use it.

Proxy dowsing in my opinion seems to employ, as I have already indicated, the mind of the operating dowser, coupled with his sample aids and his ability to fix his attention on to the proxy dowser by means of a mental/psychic link. The nearest similarity to this idea is the "aka thread" mentioned by Max Freedom Long in his book "The Secret Science at Work." This book explains his research into the operations of the Kahuna priests in Hawaii prior to 1880, i.e. before the white Christian colonists suppressed this form of religion and its remarkable powers and sincere beliefs.

I have not heard of many dowsers using the proxy method and I have seen no written articles on the subject except in the book I read. The field is wide open for research. Possibly animals could be used as proxies. I have yet to try this out. Dogs are lighter in weight than man and, for example, could possibly be sent over dangerous ground areas, such as hidden crevasses in the Arctic ice and other places that it would be unsafe to walk over.

A useful check to make when proxy dowsing is to use the sight line method of dowsing, that is, using a straight rod and sighting down it with arm extended and pointing at the distant object or area to see if a reaction can be picked up. You will find this is indicated when the end rotates and the area of reaction is sighted as that in the centre of the gyration. Obviously you have to see if it coincides with the reaction received from the proxy when you check results.

The Worcester Dowsers, of whom I am chairman, met some time ago on a hospital site, and one member explained that a main drain, which happened to be an old brick-built sewer, ran under a playing field in the grounds. Its location was not known to me, so I placed myself in a position out of sight of this playing field and asked an assistant to stand in sight of me and in sight of the proxy dowser, who was told to walk over the field. I was to shout to the assistant, who had to signal to the proxy dowser when he was to stop and to note his position accurately, as mentioned earlier. I mentally wished that the reactions from the proxy dowser should be indicated on my rod. Then by signals I ordered the proxy dowser to start his walk and also wished that the reaction be only what he received when over the hidden sewer. After a while I could feel the rod start to work (which means that the reaction is near) and when the rod reacted I shouted to the assistant to shout to the proxy dowser to stop and await my arrival to check the findings. It was a success, because we found that the position the proxy dowser stood on was over the hidden sewer, the position of which was indicated on the ground by rat holes, made by these animals which had got into the brick sewer by burrowing. Normal site dowsing over the sewer also indicated its presence, coupled with later confirmation from the site plan layout.

On another occasion, when I was engaged in weekend private flying I asked a fellow pilot friend of mine, who had never seen dowsing operated, to try an experiment while we waited on the side of the runway for our turns to pilot the club aeroplane. I asked him if he would go into the rough grass at the runway side while I turned my back and stood behind a car, and, as these grassy areas are vast, would he leave something on the ground at a point of his own choice. He was to walk anywhere and at any speed he liked, leave the object and come back to me. Off he went and I held my rod to see what happened. I fixed the wish in my mind that the rod should dip when he placed the object on the ground. After a minute or so I felt the rod dip and I awaited his return. At no time did I look round to see where he was or had been. When he returned I asked him to go back to the place where he had left the object, by whatever route he liked and at what walking speed he liked; so off he went again out of my sight and hearing. This time it seemed longer before my rod dipped and I shouted to him to stop. I called to him to return to me, and on his arrival his face was all smiles and he held out his hand in which was his penknife, the object which he had left in the grass. When I had shouted to him to stop he had picked it up only a couple of feet in front of him. Again a success and, I might say, relief to me. Had I known that he had risked losing his own penknife in grass which was then about 9 inches high it would surely have affected my concentration for fear it would never be found again.

While engaged in draining out some large lakes by dredging, I had been locating some of the feeder springs when I turned to the contractor and asked him if he had ever seen proxy dowsing in operation. He had, in fact, never seen dowsing in operation at all, so I gave a demonstration. We were at the time about 500 yards from a dam between two of the lakes, standing on rising ground. On the other side of the lake the workman operating the dredging sled had just got off the driving winch and, completely unaware of what I was doing, started walking towards the dam. I said to the contractor standing by me that I would indicate the position of the main 12 inch relief pipe which ran under the dam between the two lakes and that we would both shout to the man that he must stop and await us. The workman started to cross the dam. Again I fixed my mind on him and wished to know when he was over the pipe. After a while the rod started to move and then reacted. We yelled at him to stop and stand still till we walked down to the dam and met him in the position where he was standing. All this time we were watching him he had been unaware of our intentions. When we shouted to him to stop he faltered in his stride about four paces in all and stood still as requested. We walked down to him and noted his position, he being quite bewildered and wondering what it was all about. We allowed about 9 feet for his faltering over-run when he came to a halting stop, marked this position and looked over the dam parapet, and there just under water level was the relief pipe 4 feet away. The dam incidentally is about 150 feet long. This was a remarkably successful experiment, which was followed by much joking and laughter with the workman concerned, who wondered what it was all about, as he had been quite unaware at the time that he was involved in an experiment.

Some members of the Society who attended the 1976 Congress held at Malvern may remember the demonstration I gave to a few of them at the Holy Well site, when I showed how the straight rod responded to dowsing influences. In this instance I showed how the dowser turned into the proxy dowser. I switched as necessary to various members who were doing their individual dowse on the site and were in full view of all, and in each demonstration I stood with my back turned away from the chosen proxy dowser, who at the time was unaware that any experiment was taking place. The audience watching me noticed that my rod was circling at the same time as the proxy dowser's rod was dipping, as I said it would. There was in this case quite a lot going on all around, with members talking and dowsing, but it was no effort, in fact, relatively simple to concentrate on one of the dowsers and follow him.

One great advantage which the operating dowser has when using this method, whereby the proxy dowser walks the site, is that he has no distractions, no watching where he treads or is likely to slip and fall; he avoids the effort of walking uphill, balancing on sloping ground and the fear of sliding downhill. A second great advantage is that he need only go to the reaction point and check it himself.

Some dowsers may feel that they have no use for this method of working. Fair enough, if they rely on other methods, such as directional dowsing, another fascinating and sound method of distance dowsing, or map dowsing, etc. Use whatever method you like, but the proxy method adds to the alternative forms of dowsing which are there for the operator to use. All I can say is that it appears to work and I find it very useful when necessary. Try it yourself and I hope you are also successful. Don't be put off by failures. I have found when using this method of dowsing that at the beginning of the exercise the first try often fails. Possibly this is in anticipation of what is to come. Do a trial run over a known reaction you have located and try a few practice runs. When you seem to be getting things right, start on the serious work of locating unknown reactions. You will, so to speak, then be properly tuned in with all senses working.

Further demonstrations were carried out by me at this Congress before this talk with a fellow member, and we repeated one experiment successfully at least eight times in succession; in each case I remained out of sight of my proxy dowser. The accuracy was uncanny.

ONE MAP DOWSING TECHNIQUE EXPLAINED
Simon Stone

It is not only difficult to convince many people of the feasibility of map dowsing, but to do this by putting pen to paper and explaining one technique seems a great task if one is to remain logical and coherent. I like to keep things simple and will therefore try to explain this map dowsing procedure in simple terms. When I first became interested in map dowsing the articles which I read seemed confused and only stated what could be done and not how. I would therefore like to explain not map dowsing but one technique of it in a manner which I hope will be suitable for beginners.

The technique which I employ I call the direct method, because I hold a pendulum directly over the map, as opposed to the indirect method of holding the pendulum to one side of the map and a pointer over the map. I believe the direct method to be simpler, faster and highly accurate. V rods can also be employed for map dowsing when looking for single items or positions by intersecting live lines. A pencil alone can be used by traversing the map with it held in tightly clasped finger tips, but this method is really not very accurate.

I was little more than a beginner at rod dowsing when I tried map dowsing with a pencil and found it difficult and unreliable, very inaccurate at times, with no detail possible. I had been dealing with plans and drawings for half my life, and having learned of the results obtained by water divining from maps was determined to give it a very good trial. A friend introduced me to the pendulum, and I soon had some made and fixed to 10 inch lengths of cotton thread. That evening I convinced myself that it was possible to trace aquifers (underground streams) and plot them while doing so.

I had been asked by my employers to make a feasibility study for a borehole to provide 30,000 gallons per day during 8 hours for a district hospital laundry. So for my first job I took a 1:2500 scale plan of the 32 acre hospital site in Exeter and started dowsing. I found I could get good reactions holding the pendulum on an 8 or 9 inch thread in either hand, and these reactions could be accurately pencilled in. The pendulum is allowed to swing very slightly in the direction in which one will traverse the map with the instrument. As the pendulum approaches the aquifer the pull or swing will increase until one reaches the edge, as the bank of a river, when the pendulum will stop and be reluctant to cross this point on the map. If one wishes to proceed to the next aquifer one can mentally over-ride this reaction, but if the pendulum is held there it will start to swing in the opposite direction, the swing path having turned 90°. One can move up and down stream and repeat the process, and then on the opposite side of the aquifer by traversing in the opposite direction, and this marks both sides of the aquifer. As a check the pendulum can be made to rotate in one direction by holding it between these two lines either still or swinging slightly, thus indicating water. I traced many aquifers in this manner and site dowsing showed that an accuracy of 1 yard on the 1:2500 scale map could be obtained.

I continued working in this manner until I had almost twenty aquifers marked on the hospital plan and a large lake or concentration of water beneath the ground. The friend who had introduced me to the pendulum was blamed for not checking every aquifer but only a selection, which he had confirmed on the map later. He was asked to check my findings on site and without reference to the map he by his findings on site confirmed every aquifer which I had marked on the map. I still looked for more confirmation and months afterwards discovered the positions of six wells on the site and adjoining property, three still in existence, two filled in and one bulldozed over. I dowsed the plan in three different scales and got the same results, also from basements and ten floors high in the main block. I took adjoining O.S. maps and dowsed them also, and when held to the first sheet the aquifer, now indicated by two dotted lines, continued from one map to the other at the same angle and width.

I was now totally convinced of map dowsing and started to work on the details, such as depth. Luckily I was able to map dowse for hours on end. Depthing reached quite a satisfactory degree of accuracy from the very start by locating zones of depth and counting down. Zones of depth can easily be located on the map by first passing the pendulum over the aquifer, but I gave up locating them, as they clutter the map, take extra time to locate and are not as accurate for depthing as counting down. Bishop's Rule—driving an iron bar in the ground above the aquifer and, after touching it, walking at right angles from the aquifer for a depth reaction—can be done on the map by using a pin in place of the bar, but I found this method unreliable on the map.

There are two ways of counting down—
1. To receive an answer only on reaching the bottom depth.
2. To receive a reaction between the top and bottom depths of the water.

This also applies to map dowsing. The latter method is more informative, but it will give a reaction at depths above which a supply can be obtained. Counting down on site enables accurate depthing in confined spaces and I have a few times calculated depths down to 1200ft., but on depths up to 400ft. I can usually reach a tolerance well below 5 per cent. I believe you should only depth aquifers when one is not superimposed by another, and after checking this point, and by counting well below what you would first consider to be the bottom depth.

I believe that when discussing depths diviners should never fail to state the bottom depth, whether they give the top depth or not. Wells correctly divined and drilled should in my opinion normally be drilled right to the bottom of the aquifer, as this gives the optimum output and the most trouble-free continued supply. It should never be necessary, nor is it wise, for the diviner to add 10 to 15 per cent to his depths as a safety margin for himself, nor for the driller to allow the same tolerance, because if the impervious stratum is penetrated and gravel and/or sand lie below the supply of water can be lost. A really proficient diviner should, I feel, always check for artesian pressure, for then, depending on the porosity of the rock, it only becomes necessary to drill into the top of the aquifer.

To predetermine the quality to a limited degree is comparatively easy, at first concentrating on a yes or no reaction. Suitable for human consumption? Suitable for animal consumption? Or for irrigation or industrial use, dependent on the need? A Mager Rosette is helpful to determine this and the mineral content, etc., but once you can remember the colours of the rosette you may be ready to dispense with it. This can be done with the pendulum on the rosette and a pencil held on the aquifer, or vice versa. Whether or not one is asked to check the quality, I believe it is one's responsibility to advise on such, especially if the quality is unsuitable for the intended use and treatment plants may be required or another drilling site have to be considered. I also believe that water is a natural resource not to be spoilt or removed, that aquifers should not be run dry by over-extraction.

Quantity is by far the most difficult parameter to predetermine, and the zones of quantity to be divined outside the zones of depth on either side of the aquifer are a guide to this, but only a guide. These zones of quantity can be divined in the manner described in paragraph 4 of this article for tracing the aquifer by first passing the pendulum over the aquifer. If you use this method try 30 for the multiplying factor in place of the usual 10, but relate this to your other experience to see what factor will suit you. As with the depth zones, this method has disadvantages, and counting up is far better if it can be mastered. Count as for depth in small increments while developing your skills and take the first strong reaction, a full circle of the pendulum. Use common sense. Depths of aquifers cannot overlap and should be spaced, i.e. 50 to 60ft., 110 to 140ft., 180 to 280ft. In the same way quantity must have some relationship to size, etc.

Visit every well you can find out about, dry ones included, and divine them as for the first time; see why they were so placed and if placed correctly. On every visit you may learn one small point or just gain experience. I believe this to be much more useful to a beginner than divining reactions in the back garden and not being able to check what is there. Never ever divine by the centre of aquifers alone, because you lose one very important parameter. Most old wells were well divined but this cannot always be said of present day drillings, some of which result from wild catting, which apart from its complete failure leaves the client to pay for unnecessary depths, small quantities and unpotable quality. This at least I believe to be true of much work in Ireland, which is made worse by the most expensive diviners there are—the locals who do it for £5 or the promise of it.

Remember that competent diviners always get the same results from maps, even when divined thousands of miles from the site.

NOTES FOR BEGINNERS
Col. K.W. Merrylees

The most usual time for anyone to start an interest in dowsing is probably when he or she sees a dowser doing a survey and, with or without the dowser's assistance, tries over the same area, holding a twig or a pendulum in the same way as the dowser was seen to be doing.

If the dowser has found a flow which would be worth developing, and the newcomer finds that he obtains a perfectly genuine reaction when not assisted by the dowser, then he can consider himself sufficiently sensitive to continue his investigations—and his troubles begin.

It is my experience that while perhaps one in twenty persons is sufficiently sensitive naturally to get a recognisable reaction over a good, well-defined indication, not more than one per cent. of these are naturally so sensitive that they can expect to receive and distinguish all the important indications without a long and laborious development of sensitivity. This does not mean that this "supersensitive" one per cent. are already capable dowsers. They are as far from it as the schoolboy finding himself gifted with a good "eye" for games is from becoming a Wimbledon class tennis player. I believe it is possible for almost anyone

55

with a small initial sensitivity to develop this gift, but there seems to be a minimum receptivity without which certain essential indications are not received, and therefore full and reliable results cannot be obtained.

If we agree that, apart from experience, the dowser must have this important minimum, then it is quite clear that only the most persevering and serious-minded persons, finding their initial reactions small, should continue dowsing, unless they are prepared to spend laborious years on known flows and " local disturbances," only then venturing to give predictions for the costly operation of well sinking.

I am therefore only addressing two categories of aspiring dowsers: one, the small percentage of the one per cent. " naturals " who are willing to learn all they should before they practice, and two, the very much smaller number of those whose natural sensitivity is small but who have great patience and perseverance, and an adequate gift of commonsense and self-control.

I would discourage no one from developing and using such a useful gift, but I hope that the time will come soon when the word " dowsing " and " magic " are no longer related in the public mind and, in consequence, dowsing may become something which is recognised generally and respected as being the result of training and experience as well as the use of a natural gift. The selection of a pilot to fly an aircraft depends on physical characteristics such as good eyesight and a sense of balance, but there is a long and strict training in the application of these physical attributes ; yet there are dowsers practising with little natural gift and no careful training, but who would be aghast if they were asked to pilot an aircraft with no further qualifications than that they could ride a bicycle.

Elsewhere I have advocated the necessity for the study of geology and hydrology for all dowsers, and here I propose to describe one method of carrying out a survey though I seem, by my above remarks, to have reduced my readers to a very small number.

I will not attempt to try to explain the dowsing phenomenon, but it is, I think, almost universally agreed that the final result of the dowser passing over a " local disturbance " is a movement of his twig, pendulum or other indicator, and that this movement is directly caused by the involuntary movement of some of the dowser's muscles. Theoretically all dowsers should receive the same sort of indications in the same spots, whatever the indicator used. In practice this does not always seem so, but provided the result of the deductions made from the indications is the same this does not matter very much.

I hope that later on we may know enough of the cause or the reactions on the human receiver for us to discard all but certain reliable indications and methods. I believe that the development of the human receiver into an intelligent automaton, unswayed by auto-suggestion or psychological influences, is a most desirable objective, though I also consider that a condition of mental receptivity—not mere " concentration "—is essential to satisfactory reception. " Mental receptivity " is a little difficult to describe. Apart from the physical act of tensing the arm, and probably other muscles, I find that I am imagining what, from my geological information, might exist beneath the surface, and am visualizing mentally the aquifer or flow. I am never disappointed when my indications show differences from this picture, since that shows that I am not " auto-suggesting " results.

To take a simple case and describe the " drill " which I would normally use, I will assume that Farmer A has asked me to examined a field, roughly level, of ten acres or so. I must assume that I have been through the essential preliminary studies of geology and rainfall statistics of the catchment area in which the field lies, and that I have thereby satisfied myself that the water could be there.

On arriving at the field I would set out to walk along at least three of the field's boundaries, using a round section, 14in. whalebone twig which I hold horizontal at waist level, and carrying a few of the labelling pegs used by gardeners. The good point about whalebone is that it is almost unbreakable, and that its springiness remains unaltered in any climate. I can find no advantage in any special dress or shoes, colour of twig or similar idiosyncrasy, direction of walk, time of day or (at this stage) use of samples ; but I would not therefore say that such aids, which I believe to be purely psychological, are not of use to some people. It may be that I just inhibit their use by not believing in their value to me.

If there is an aquifer beneath the field, I get warning by a feeling of " liveliness " in the twig as soon as I start moving. This is followed, if I am approaching a subsoil flow in the aquifer, by a gradual lift of the twig as I near the first band. At this point I can quote an account which appeared in the *B.S.D. Journal*, Vol. II, 15, p. 307 (1936) :

" The next indication is a straight pull down, when I at once stop and take a new grip with the twig, again horizontal. Within a pace or two, the twig still being " alive," it will lift to about 45°, and then turn until vertically downwards. This is usually quite a sharp movement. Taking another grip, a yard or two further on there is again a sharp single downward pull. These three

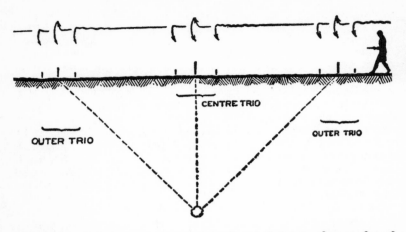

CENTRE TRIO

OUTER TRIO

OUTER TRIO

indications I have named a "trio," and I have always found three such trios connected with every flow of water below ground.

So far I do not know if this first trio is that belonging to the stream itself, or if it is one of the two symmetrical outer trios. Also I do not know at what angle I am approaching the stream. I therefore return to the centre indication of the trio, and standing on this I slowly rotate with the twig held normally. When facing in two opposite directions the twig will drop. This is the general direction of the flow of the stream at this point, and it is possible to walk away at right angles to this directional line and so find the shortest way to the next "trio." Still I do not know which "trio" belongs to the stream itself, and one of two tests is now applied. Again standing in the centre of the trio, and facing in either of the found directions, I hold the twig with my hands close to the ground. If the twig lifts or drops it is the stream itself, and the direction of the flow is from the direction in which I am facing when the twig lifts. Similarly, and this is a better test, if I walk along the indicated direction of the stream and the twig lifts or drops, then it is truly the stream. The outer trios produce no indication with this test."

Having now fixed the position of the flow in two places on the boundaries of the site, it is usual to find that a third flow-centre must be found so placed that it is possible to walk out in two directions normal to the direction of flow at this point. This is done so as to allow room for a standard "Creyke" depth test on both sides of the flow and, as I always prefer it, at right angles to the flow.

The "Creyke" method of depthing* is based on the formation

* See *B.S.D.J.*, II, **16**, p. 353.

of a " field " round a metal rod which is placed upright on the centre band. This rod appears to cause a field round it, roughly circular and distant from the rod the approximate depth to flow or aquifer. As there appears to be some refraction of this field, depending on the subsoil strata, a correction factor is nearly always necessary.

I think that many errors in depthing are made because the dowser stops after the first one or two aquifer depth indications, whereas the flow depth may be greater still, and I therefore prefer to walk a long way beyond any possible depth indication to make quite sure that I have covered them all. I think that the special mumetal rod may give a better result than similar sized rods of other metals, but I have not attempted to compare them carefully.

As I have already measured the triple-band widths at both the original crossing places, and as the width of these bands is related to the quantity of water flowing, I have now only to apply such correction factors as I think fit and I have position, depth and quantity. I do not think one dowser's correction factors can be applied by another to his own measurements, and it is therefore up to each dowser to produce his own correction factors from measurements over known flows, but preferably flows of which he has no detailed information before he starts.

Finally, the conscientious dowser will return to the site on a later occasion and do the whole operation over again away from the points on the flow line that he has already used.

If the dowser is lucky he will now be able to examine records of local wells and by not seeing such records until he has finally made up his mind from his own search, he will be able to get a much better idea of what his errors, if any, are.

If there is a suspicion that the aquifer it is proposed to use is saline, a comparative test with samples of various strengths of solution can be made, but this involves comparing differences in neuro-muscular reflexes which, unless acute, are, in my opinion, extremely difficult to assess.

There are many pitfalls into which the inexperienced dowser may fall but which can mostly be eliminated with little trouble. Certain " local disturbances " may produce reactions very similar to parts of the flow indications. For example, it is not unusual to find faults and flows adjacent to one another, or pipes and cables within the surface pattern of the flow which is being examined. Practice over known faults, pipes, &c., can be very easily obtained, as suitable vertical faults can be found from the sections on the geological maps, and manholes or the local water or electricity authorities can indicate pipes or cables. There is, I know, a danger of over-confidence once some of the " local

59

disturbances " have been practised upon, but care will nearly always eliminate error. The irregularity of alignment of natural formations is usually in distinct contrast to the straight lines associated with man-made foundations, tunnels, pipelines, &c.

The above describes the simplest type of survey. Almost inevitably the dowser will find some conditions which he has not met before—sloping ground, dip of strata, hidden faults, power cables, steel buildings, or uncontrollable factors such as a curious crowd, or changes in the sunspot cycle—all or any of which may have some effect on his results and the corrections which he applies. Equally inevitably he will develop his own methods, which it is quite correct that he should do, since he is using his own brain and body as a super-sensitive recording instrument.

BEWARE OF GHOSTS
H. Guttridge

When I first became interested in dowsing I was beset by several trials, the sort of thing which a writer in the Journal described as " the dogged finding of what is never there at all."

I was not then interested in water divining; there were plenty of experts on that. But I felt there were many ways in which dowsing could be useful in building and civil engineering. In fact, I cannot understand why any man who digs a hole in a street or in a field doesn't have a dowsing rod in his pocket. He could save himself or his employers pounds—perhaps even thousands of pounds.

At first, however, I ran into so many difficulties that I wondered whether dowsing was accurate enough to be of practical use. My first problem is set forth in the sketch. It was a site at Doncaster. I approached the Council and City Engineer and enquired whether there were any drains running in this road. They turned up all their maps but they couldn't tell me where any of the drains from the houses went to. At that time I had just borrowed an angle rod and I thought that might give me the answer. We wanted a drain supply on Site A. There were manholes at B and C, as shown, and it was natural to assume that between those two manholes there was a sewer, and all I had to do was to cross the road and find the drain. I walked out into the road and I got a reaction, so I marked the spot. Then I made another approach a short distance away, and again the rods turned. I made approaches all the way along and each time the rods turned. Finally we put on an ordinary builder's line, pulled it tight, and it passed through the centre of all those markers. " There's the sewer," we thought,

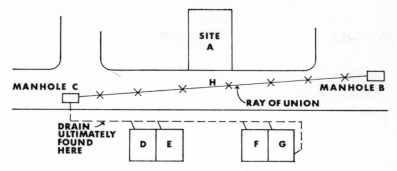

but when we took the manhole covers off and looked inside there was no drain there in the position indicated.

On the second site we were going to erect a very big building in a field, and we wanted to know where the drain went from a road gully. We knew there was a manhole with a cover 10ft. deep and we thought the drain would come across to this manhole. I took my angle rods and at certain points they turned, both of them. Now in my dowsing career I have been fortunate in that there has always been an excavator available, so that I could whip out a big hole in a matter of minutes. I had a trench dug 14ft. deep at a point on the line of reaction; it went through virgin clay and there was no sign of a drain. I then had a hole dug alongside the road gully and found that the drain ran in an entirely different direction from the line of reaction. This was the second failure and it was very worrying.

On another site we were to take over a lead water pipe from the Coal Board. It had taken the solicitors two years to obtain permission for us to make a connection to a water pipe, which was in the old switch house of a colliery. When I got there after the two years the power station had been flattened to the ground and all the hard core had been levelled out, 14ft. deep. And there was a lead pipe underneath! Actually the Coal Board Manager had worked a fast one on us. He thought we were going to connect our toilet to his water pipe, so, just before we finished the building, he chopped the pipe off. He wanted us to take over the lead main that ran from this toilet to his pit, a distance of two miles. We took it over but we couldn't find the pipe. We dug and dug and I traced with my little angle rods, using samples. I came to a place where a line ran for 20 or 30 yards perfectly straight, which gave every indication of being of lead. I dug a trench there as deeply as the excavator would go, and it was pure yellow clay. A man who had worked in the pit as a boy told me, " We used to let the pit ponies out in the field, but there was never a water pipe down there." So we filled it in and sent for an expert dowser. He walked across and his rods turned in the same place, and he said, "There's the water pipe." We put a line down and it was in a straight line. We dug down and there was nothing there. "Ah," he said. "That's what we call remanence." Now I could see from the unbroken nature of that clay that it was there as it had been laid down; there had never been any pipe there.

I thought, "There's something strange here. We're getting a reaction in an area where we know there can't be a lead pipe." I said to the digger, "We'll start here and we'll inspect every bucketful that you bring out." At the first point we found a big stone which was terribly heavy. I had never found such a heavy stone. We put it on one side. We went down to the far end and there we found another of these big stones. I didn't need to take it to a geologist; it was obvious from the weight that it had lead in it. I don't know where it had come from. It wasn't remanence that was giving the reactions, it was two big stones. We took those two stones away, and then wherever we went we could get very little reaction. Ultimately we found the lead pipe, but that is another story.

At that time I worked for the Electricity Board at Wakefield. When they heard of my interest in dowsing and that I was going to patent a new form of angle rod, they thought there might be something in it for them and wanted a demonstration. I said, "Yes, on one condition. It must be done in a virgin field, away from all other buildings, where there can be no interference. And first the land must be walked over by a dowser, so that all the dowsing reactions are marked on the ground." "Oh no," they said. "We won't have anything to do with that. It wouldn't be a test. But we will use a virgin field." They said they would bury a lot of objects—pieces of cable, pipes, all sorts of things, and I could find them. This they did and the great day dawned. It was all kept hush hush and secret from me. The chief engineers and others came down. They led the way in their cars and I followed in mine. We went into an urban area and drew into a yard where there was a little tiny plot of land surrounded by buildings in which there was all the electrical apparatus you could imagine, and in this bit of land they had buried all that stuff. To my own knowledge the land was full of cables before they had ever started. I was on the point of giving up, but they said, "This is the sort of area where we may have to use the abilities you claim." So I went round the area and found all sorts of things, but every time I found something they looked at their drawings and said, "Oh no, that isn't anything we buried." I said, "No? Well, there are all sorts of other things." At last I said, "Why don't you all forget it and go home?" So they went home and I went home as well.

While I sat having my tea I thought about an experiment we

used to do at school. We took two magnets, and put a piece of paper on the top. We scattered iron filings around, but in between the magnets we had a little iron ring on top of the paper. This little iron ring was a screen. As we scattered the iron filings all over the paper they formed lines all over the place, but when they reached the ring in the centre they stayed as dots on the paper. All the filings on the outside clutched around, together with the field of the magnet, but the little dots in the centre didn't move. I wondered whether this would work for dowsing.

I got a piece of iron wire and went straight back to the site. I put the iron wire on the ground in the form of a ring and walked inside it. It acted as a shield and I no longer picked up extraneous things. Next morning I couldn't get out to the place fast enough. I laid down my shield and walked inside it. As soon as I started walking the rods closed together, both of them. Now if you hold a piece of iron in a certain way, in an upright position, in the right hand of an angle rod, you will prevent the rod being affected by iron. So I got a nail and held that in my hand, and wherever I walked inside the shield the rods didn't move. Then I walked outside the shield and they did turn. When people saw what I was doing they came out of the house and said, " There's a little manhole cover buried under our garden there." So I knew I had got an answer to the problem.

I started reading up about dowsing, and in book after book I saw references to the ray of union. Abbé Mermet in " Practice and Principles of Radiesthesia " refers to it as the witness ray, and describes how a witness object can be used to locate the position of a hidden object of the same material. " When passing over a ray of union between two objects," he writes, " the dowsing instruments react in the same sure manner as they would were a length of the actual material to be in the ground." You often hear people talk about " ghosting " or about " remanence," where a thing has been in the ground and is there no longer. It is my belief that what you get is the ray of union.

I found out an interesting thing in a garden. Two little children were playing about where we were doing some dowsing. I gave them two angle rods and they went up the garden. When they got halfway up the rods turned. They came back and I sent them up the garden again, and again the rods turned. I was puzzled for a moment, then I said, " There's a very big lupin plant on one side of the path and another one on the other side. Get that length of hosepipe, join the ends together and put it down on the ground to form a path and walk inside it." I gave them a piece of hosepipe to hold in the right hand. They did that and they no longer picked up the lupin plants.

You get a very strong dowsing reaction between any kind of tree and any kind of plant of the same species, as sure and certain as though you were walking over quite a good stream, and it is only due to the ray of union. I was interested one day to read on pages 382 and 383 of Journal 52 a letter from Mr. Busby of Cowra, New South Wales, in which he wrote: " I have observed that every tree of any distinct variety appears to have a peculiar connection with others of the same variety, though not with others of the same genus . . . This ' line of communication ' can be easily traced with a rod, particularly the angle rod type, even over a considerable distance. I have traced them for several hundreds of yards when certain specimens were growing at that distance apart."

This I think is of vital importance, because many a time you can find clear indications of a dowsing reaction, only to find nothing alien there when you dig. If a piece of hosepipe is laid on a clear area to form a shield you will pick up nothing outside that, but you must neutralise the shield itself or you will pick that up. All you need is a little bit of the material in the right hand, whether you use the angle rods or the V rod. I call this hosepipe a magnetic shield. Of course, it isn't, but it behaves like one. I personally would never dream of digging or saying with certainty that an object was in the ground, unless first of all I had walked inside that shield. Suppose you are in the garden looking for a drain. There would be a path, and all at once you would think you had found the drain. You would dig and there would be no drain there. Along the edge of the path there might be a border made of fireclay blocks—very old-fashioned ones with a little roll over the top of them, made of salt glazed earthenware—exactly the same stuff as a drain. You could get a reaction from one of those and think it was a drain.

Here I would like to mention dowsing tests, because that is something that gets my goat. I read an article in one of the Journals about a most magnificent test carried out in which members of our Society took part. They were looking for " mines." About 400 holes were dug; a lot of them were filled with bits of wood and concrete, and the conclusion in " Nature " was that the findings were no better than chance. Most tests are of value, because you have to convince somebody, but before any members take part again I would advise that the ground be gone over first by a competent dowser to mark the position in a permanent manner of every dowsing reaction that he finds. What is the use of people burying half drums of salt water and half drums of plain water where there are boulders and all sorts of things that will give dowsing reactions? It is just stupid. It can only be done by having grid lines laid and the dowser following the grid line, so that he is following a straight line all the time and can find all the reactions. Then they can start to lay the objects. Nobody in our Society should be persuaded to go in for that sort of test unless it is properly done, otherwise it will be a failure.

The original premises of the British Society of Dowsers, as stated at the beginning of Maby and Franklin's book, are as true today as when they were written all those years ago. They tell you that if you use samples of materials you will only find the same material as the samples. All we are doing when we use samples is creating rays of union. Some dowsers might prefer to use colours, because each article, each material, has its own wavelength in colour. Whether we use samples or colours, we are both doing the same thing. If you carry samples of pipe glaze, salt or ceramic, for example, you will get no reaction from a copper pipe. I use hollow boxes for finding voids. You can put them on any form of dowsing instrument and, whatever you walk over, you will get no reaction unless the object is hollow.

By deliberately creating a "ghost" i.e. using a witness, it is possible to make a search of large areas for hidden objects, even where there are many buildings, by working on one side of the area at a time. The approximate position of the hidden object can be found either by triangulation or by following the ray of union created.

My procedure is a purely physical one and may, according to the nature of the site being searched, involve extensive use of samples. Normally a sufficient number of opposing samples must be used to prevent angle rods being influenced by other rays of union which may be in the vicinity, other than the one in which there is an interest, or specially prepared angle rods may be used which will only turn when an object of the same material as the witness is encountered. A witness is placed on the ground on one side of the site. Using angle rods or V rods, the operator circles around the object, about 6ft. away from it. Should another object containing material similar to the witness be in the vicinity, at some point the ray of union will be intercepted and the rods will turn as they do when an actual object such as a pipe has been located under foot. A mark is now made on the ground at this spot and another on the position occupied by the witness. Then the witness is moved some distance away and the process repeated. Lines are then drawn passing through the witness and the reaction point; the two lines will cross at some place and the hidden object should be found thereabouts.

Alternatively, you may find one ray of union and leave the witness in position. Then the ray can be followed in exactly the same manner as the course of a pipe in the ground is followed. When the hidden object is reached both rods will turn. It will be remembered that when following the course of a pipe or cable the rods will either turn inwards, forming a cross, or outwards, forming a V (according to the polarity of the operator), the cross or V being equal so long as the operator is over the pipe.

The matter of rays of union seems to me of great importance and something which should be constantly kept in mind when dowsing.

Finally, I would like to tell you how I once looked for gold on a Yorkshire farm. A man rang up from Harrogate and said, " I'll pay you £5 if you will come and see if there is any gold on my farm." It was a nice afternoon and I thought, " Why throw £5 away?" So I went over there and he took me into his beautiful new farmhouse. He said, " Before I bought this farm it belonged to an old gentleman. His brother had left him a farm, so he had the proceeds of two farms, and when he died very little money was in the estate. He always said that the land had made the money and when he died the money would go back to the land. I pulled the old farmhouse down to within 3ft. of the ground but I have found no gold. I have looked all over the farm—everywhere. I wouldn't mind now if somebody would tell me positively that there isn't any gold."

We went outside and I placed a witness of gold in a tin on the ground. I fastened a sample of gold to my angle rods and walked in a circle round the witness. I got a reaction and he was very excited. I followed the line, which led through a long building and outside again to a big pile of rubbish—straw, pieces of wood, baling string and one thing and another. " Do you know," he said, " there's a well under there. I bet he put it down that well." I said, " We must pinpoint the exact spot." I got several lines from different directions and they all pointed to the rubbish heap. Then he said. " I've just remembered. We had a girl who kept her pony in a stable here. I put all the rubbish from the stable on that heap. One day that girl lost her engagement ring somewhere around here." I said, " It's in that lot there." It was getting near dinnertime in winter and I said, " I haven't time to go through all that. Get your tractor and we'll clean it up." So he swept it all up and took it down the bottom of the field. And as soon as he did that the ray of union disappeared.

I went all round the farm buildings and now got no reactions until we were back at the first building we had passed. " That's funny," I said, " I never got a signal here before." The farmer called out his wife's name and she popped out of the building (she had gone in unseen by us to get corn for the hens), and she had a gold ring on her finger!

I continued to search but found nothing else. In the end the farmer said he was very pleased to know for certain that there was no gold there. He said, " It's all been very well worth it and I shall never worry about it again."

DOWSING APPLIED TO ARCHITECTURE
Clive Thompson

The subject of my paper is mainly related to practical dowsing on building sites with special reference to architectural matters although I will add a number of experiences I have had in dealing with archaeological sites. My work as an architect naturally involves me in surveying and building over many sites of different character, varying from those on virgin soil to those located in highly built up areas. The survey of sites on virgin land, especially in the open countryside, is by far the simplest, and the sites can be dowsed easily by using map-dowsing techniques or by resorting to field dowsing (or a combination of both), a square search being the most thorough method to adopt.

Sites which have been built upon, some of which have an archaeological history, are obviously the more complicated. It is advisable therefore, before commencing with surveys on ground of this nature, to obtain as much information as possible regarding previous building works from authentic sources in order that one can plan the work and draw up a map of the site. The more you know of the hidden objects below the surface the lighter will be your task of analysing the reactions felt while dowsing and thus heighten the chance of a sure and accurate dowsing survey.

The method I generally adopt for all site dowsing surveys (after I have obtained the known information) is first to map dowse the plans at the office, make notes, draw my plottings on them and then visit the site to see if the forecasting has proved correct. Should I prove correct in the information I want, I then generally carry on with a square search, using a rod to see if I have missed anything. If I have proved incorrect in the map-dowsing, I must then obviously obtain all the information from the site itself. To date my map dowsing has been 60%-70% accurate, although I have not been able yet to depth accurately enough by map dowsing techniques alone.

The main problem facing architects, engineers and contractors on sites, has always concerned the nature and content of the subsoil; whether natural or man-made. Natural subsoils can vary considerably from alluvial or clay soils, to rocky formations (or a combination of both). Some of course have natural water tables, underground streams, voids and fissures or simply nothing of this nature at all, but sound unimpeded subsoil to receive foundations and services. Foundations and services are required by all buildings, whether they are to be built or are already in existence and any prior knowledge the architect, engineer or contractor can obtain before site works commence on subsoil contents will help to prevent trouble and thus save costs. This section of the building programme is often the most complicated and costly in its structural form and the client or general public will not see the work that has been carried out once it is buried in the ground.

The general work in connection with buildings that are hidden below the ground consists of foundations, ducts, wells, cisterns, sewers, drains (of all types), culverts, basements and plant rooms, tunnels, manholes, service pipes (such as water, gas and heating pipes), electrical or telephone conduits and buried obstructions; either man-made or natural (which may often be of an archaeological nature). All of which must be located or put in, either at the planning stage (if possible), or discovered and dealt with when site work is in progress. Not only are problems limited to levels below ground but they may be buried within building structures above ground. These problems are generally met with when engaged in altering or enlarging existing buildings and often turn up in the most unexpected positions. They may often be very difficult to deal with when come upon if their existence has not been previously detected.

In general, all the natural and man-made obstacles can be detected by dowsing methods. Some are harder to find and there are many instances where more than one are located in an area. Practical experience and dowsing methods, coupled with a specialised knowledge of building, is the only way to analyse what can be detected. The systems I use to distinguish between one influence and another is a combination of common sense and analysis using samples, colours, fundamental directions based on magnetic north and a numbering system based on the rod reactions. In order to dowse certain influences I personally find that one type of dowsing instrument will not adequately serve all purposes, so it has been necessary for me to find out the limitations of each instrument and choose the most suitable according to circumstances. Sometimes I use more than one if necessary.

The instruments I use can be any of the following: a simple, neutral-black pendulum, hollowed to take samples; a range of coloured pendulums of equal weight; a straight plastic rod; a light weight flat whale bone rod; a light weight $\frac{1}{8}$in. square sectioned whalebone rod; a pair of steel angle rods and a double ' V ' whalebone rod (a type of rod I recently developed, the details of which I will mention later). To assist me in map dowsing I use a Mager Rosette in conjunction with a neutral or coloured pendulum.

To my knowledge the only way adopted by contractors and engineers to find pipes and conduits, is to use equipment which relies on the picking up of electro-magnetic waves induced into the pipes, which incidentally must be made of metal, otherwise there is no reliable indication. Only in the rare instance have

68

contractors and men any knowledge of dowsing methods, although some have seen them used when water is being sought; or when a rod has been used by electricians who may have used angle rods to find their conduits and wires. Dowsing is not widely used on sites and the majority of dowsers are not consulted when problems occur, so it appears to me that the field is wide open in the contracting world for the sound application of dowsing methods. These can only be beneficial if properly used. Over the last twelve or so years since I became really interested in dowsing, I have applied a growing knowledge and skill in this art to my work. I have had my successes and my failures and a number of case histories might be of interest to you at this juncture.

For example, while engaged in deepening a basement near the centre of Bristol some years ago, it was known that an old sewer ran underneath. The position was not marked on existing plans. I decided during a site visit early in the alteration work, to dowse this and plot it on site and on to the working drawing. The reactions of the sewer line were so definite that I plotted it on the floor and instructed the foreman to form the new manhole taking the new drains from a certain point and joining them to the sewer at another point. All the connections were chalked on the basement floor. I then depthed the sewer and told the foreman to proceed. When I next visited the site I found all the forecasted connections made and the men in a happy co-operative mood, they having much enjoyed the experiment.

While I was staying at an hotel in Bristol about five years ago, I noticed that the driveway to an adjacent building had been dug up and that the workmen were standing in a long trench with water in the bottom. On enquiring I was told that they were trying to find a water main which was leaking. The water board official in charge had indicated the line of the pipe with an induction coil but it still had not been found. As I had my whalebone rod to hand I traversed the trench and adjacent driveway and located the pipe about 9in. away from one of the trench sides and showed this to the men. While the foreman was in the house turning off the interrupter which he had fixed in order to use the induction coil, one of the workmen using his pickaxe plunged it into the trench side where I told him the pipe was and after two strokes, brought it out of the side of the trench much to the amusement of his colleagues. I left the site before the foreman returned to face his men.

About four years ago, soon after I had learned to map dowse, I was engaged on alteration work on a re-build job in Weston-super-Mare where an existing basement was dug out and a new one was being put in. To those unfamiliar with this area, Weston-super-Mare is a seaside town on the south side of the Bristol Channel near the Severn estuary. The subsoil near the sea is subject to a tidal water table and for this reason there are few basements to be found in the town. Sheet piling was used to hold the excavation back in anticipation of trouble. While all this work was in hand under the direction of a local architect, it occurred to me that I might map dowse the plans and see what I could find before first visiting the site. I map dowsed on a drawing at my London office and noted that there was a strong influence, possibly a watercourse, that under-ran the building. Also, there was a strong point of influence in an area of the basement. I went on site and found the reactions I expected and mentioned these to the local architect, and the foreman told me I was right. They had hit a spring and uncovered an old well while excavating. Old town records found later indicated that there had been a cress bed under the line of the shops.

A professional colleague at my office showed me a plan of a building where the drainage lines were missing and indicated the position of a toilet on the ground floor. There was also no indication of manholes or sewers in the roadway or on the pavement. His problem was to find the drainage line from this toilet to the sewer connection from the building and he asked me if I could map-dowse this. I traced the line of this fitting to the sewer line and marked it on the drawing and he took it to the site with him. When next we met he told me that they dug where I had indicated the drain would be and they had found it.

Although this is not my own personal experience as the event happened to a contractor friend of mine, I think it is worth recounting here. I was involved in erecting a temporary wooden building on a car park site in Weston-super-Mare some years ago. This site had once accommodated a cinema which had been pulled down and the ground had been levelled and covered with cinders. This building, like all others, required a water service and records were consulted at the Town Hall indicating where the main ran in the street; no indication being shewn of a water pipe in the area of the car park. My colleague, a dowser himself, using a whalebone rod, found the old rising main connection in the street that had served the cinema and traced it to a point where it terminated under the cinders in the car park. The men dug at the point indicated and they found the old water meter. A new main was connected from this old connection and the rising main taken to the temporary building. A saving indeed in cost and time with no pavement excavation.

The cases I have mentioned are just a few of the many in which I have been involved and it would take a long time to describe them all. As I have already mentioned, each site often produces a problem which can be solved by dowsing. Some are very small and simple; others are more complicated. Being able to dowse whilst doing my particular work I feel very fortunate in that I can constantly apply this gift and without much trouble see the results of my forecasts either emerge correct or false. Each time this happens I learn something. I think that one outstanding incident in my early life convinced me of the value of being able to locate hidden springs and other entities. This was when I was a schoolboy at Harrogate before the war, about 1936/7. The incident occurred on a site where contractors were digging out ground to form the basement of the Regal cinema. While excavations were in hand a mineral spring was struck, causing flooding which held up work. I believe this spring is either now diverted or is one of many which is now piped to the Remedial Baths in the town.

The occurrence of sites being temporarily flooded by unknown springs, watercourses and uncharted drains is all too frequent and has generally been experienced by all contractors at some time or another. The worst case I have known is where a site in Dover had the basement excavations flooded when on old uncharted brick sewer was broken into by the excavator and the diggings were covered with foul sewage. You can imagine the rest. A common occurrence on existing sites, especially house properties, is the digging of holes by workmen. Ask them what they are doing, and invariably they reply that they are looking for a service pipe. Ask again if they know where to find it, and it is either " Yes, it is shewn on the plans " or " No but it is somewhere here." In the latter case you must agree, a very hit and miss arrangement and ripe for dowsing methods to be applied to solve the problem.

As you will have noted from what I have already mentioned, dowsing used for architectural problems is essentially a practical application of the art to site problems and as far as I can determine, at present, this is the full extent to which it can be used. To apply dowsing methods to planning and other architectural problems without a practical application does not appear to help one. The application of dowsing methods to building problems, other than the finding of water, has much to offer in the saving of time, labour and money and it surprises me that more use has not been made of the professional dowser for this purpose, or that those in the contracting world, whether on a large or small scale, have not troubled to study the art. Dowsing knowledge can be traced in some form or other to Egyptian times where the records show that an Egyptian engineer or architect used the rod. With all unfathomable phenomena, a category into which dowsing unfortunately still falls, those engaged in its study and application have a struggle for recognition by the ordinary man and still more so from the scientific specialist who only rigidly accepts pure proven scientific facts.

I feel that the main basis for the acceptance of the dowser is the very nature and application of his work. It is highly personal and responsive to his trained mind and natural bodily reactions. Yet its methods follow scientific reasoning much of the way until the tables turn and it seems to disobey or go outside known scientific facts. This is far too puzzling to the general run of scientists but is a constant challenge to those interested in dowsing ever seeking its secrets.

While dowsing over the years I have come to accept various rods and other instruments to help me locate the reactions I seek. I am not gifted like a number of natural dowsers to feeling reactions without the need of a dowsing rod etc., I find that the heavy rods, used by some, are far too powerful and tiresome to use, and so I prefer light rods. Some dowsers say you should only utilise one instrument. I do not however find this but suggest that you should try all methods and master them and find their limitations. In other words, widen your dowsing instrument vocabulary.

There is a brief description summarised from my notes by the Editor in the B.S.D. Journal, September, 1967.

I hope the above notes may be helpful to some people for I feel that much work can be done by the Society in finding out the methods etc., we all use. I am forever experimenting with ideas either thought out long ago by others, or trying something new to see if they will work. The pattern they take, their limitations and how they fit into the overall dowsing sequences. However all seems to point to a basic procedure I mentioned earlier that archaeological site dowsing enters into my field of work as most of this subject deals with the remains of buildings or is appertaining to ancient buildings. These often take the form of voids, tunnels, wells, foundations, or simply filled in man-made holes in the ground, apart from objects left in the ground, and these can be found in the most unexpected places, especially on sites of an historical nature.

On the 15th August last year I visited the site of Camelot at Castle Cadbury in Wiltshire and while I was looking over the site of the dig I demonstrated how the holes the archaeological searchers were uncovering, could be easily detected by the straight rod over the untouched turf surface of the ground and I was shown in return by the survey team on site, how they forecast the position of the holes and undulations in the rock face below the ground by the use of a special electronic broadcast machine. The square survey pattern of these had been plotted on a map of the whole site and had proved very accurate. However, during the dig the team had uncovered in their section of the site what appeared to be a zig-zag trench which the machine had not forecast. I then with a member of the site team dowsed the line

72

of the trench outside the area of the dig and showed him the positions and these were roughly marked out. This has now been verified as correct as trial digs have been made and reported in the Sunday Observer Supplement although no mention was made of the dowser who helped them find what appears to be the site of a very ancient church (?) and which is to be the first exercise of this year's dig when it will be exploited for all to see. Is the dowser still a mystery man?

The final experience I will relate here refers to my appearance last autumn on Westward television (" Westward Diary ") and this relates to a successful exercise in map dowsing in front of recording cameras etc. I was asked by Westward television if I would be willing to show how streams could be found using a map and so the stage was set. Unknown to me while travelling by car on the 27th June last year to Yeovil, the recording team were in Yeovil during the morning of the day I was due and recorded on their cameras the commentator coming out of a hole in the road near the parish church. This hole had been dug by the council for the purpose of building a culvert. They had struck while engaged on this work, a strong flow of water which was now flooding the works and pumps were in operation to deal with this. I arrived in Yeovil by a roundabout route (not through the town) to the office of a local architect friend and found the television team and the deputy borough engineer awaiting me. I knew nothing of what was in hand or what I had to find. After lunch I was led to a table in front of the cameras, interviewed by the commentator and told I was to find an underground stream that ran near the parish church. Using a square search with the pendulum with a violet sample I located a reaction on the map and finished with plotting a line across the map running under the corner of the church, across the street below the former. The commentator, looking rather astounded, said my line crossed the hole he had been in that morning where the stream had been discovered. This recorded film was put on Westward television on " Westward Diary " on the 15th August, 1967, one of the features after the news. During the evening after the recording was made I visited the site with my professional colleague and found my map dowsing line was about dead on to the line of the influence I could detect with a rod. This I relate as a typical case where map or site dowsing could have saved the council trouble on its sites and workings.

In all dowsing work it appears that the intuitive senses are at work and that basic selection is carried out by the brain which must be trained to accept what it receives from outside influences through various parts of the body (with the assistance, as necessary, of dowsing instruments). The indications must be unquestioned and only analysed by the brain. All this takes time, training and concentration. The best concentration is found when one is engrossed in the search despite the inevitable distractions; for these are the conditions one has to put up with in site dowsing, especially when dealing with building sites which cannot be kept quiet and peaceful and one is constantly in conversation with those around; even when dowsing. I hope my talk will interest others who may be engaged on architectural, archaeological or other similar work.

VERY PRACTICAL DOWSING
H. Guttridge

My occupation is that of Clerk of Works and I often make use of dowsing to locate the position of drains, cables, pipes, conduits, etc., and to determine their composition after location. I have also found dowsing of use in finding the position of leakages in water pipes and drains.

I have carried out a great amount of research into dowsing particularly concerning angle rods.

The methods I use are in my opinion the best for my particular purpose and they can be used by anyone possessing some degree of dowsing sensitivity. I find them very accurate and after all the proof of the pudding is in the eating, particularly when it is Yorkshire pudding.

I think more people than is commonly realised could become dowsers but, as is the case with all tools, some degree of manual dexterity is required, we all probably know someone who is unable to knock a nail in straight.

I believe that basically the dowsing phenomenon is of purely physical origin but I know from experience that mental processes can quite easily become part of ones dowsing practice, if one allows them to do so.

It is also possible to become interested in such things as word witnesses, colour samples, mental inhibitions, serial numbers, foot tapping, etc., and before you know where you are you are all mixed up and nothing seems to work right. Dowsing starts by being simple, it is only we dowsers who make it complicated.

When I first became interested in dowsing I thought that my dowsing sensitivity must be weak, the vee rod would not apparently work in my hands. Several dowsers had allowed me to try to use their rods but without success. I was not unduly concerned, at that time my angle rods would do all that I wanted but when, following an operation, I found my angle rods sensitivity soon became exhausted I again turned my attention to the vee rod. I visited our member Mrs. Myers and she kindly gave me a small privet twig to practice with. When I returned home I sat in my chair and played with this twig, bending it in all directions and varying the muscular pressure. I did this for several nights and then suddenly the penny dropped, what the dowsers had not stressed was how necessary it is to bring the rod into the state of unstable equilibrium. I liken this to the cocking of a gun, all you then have to do is to walk along and on passing over the edge the radiation from the object will trigger it off.

Since then I have shewn many people how to use a vee rod with few failures but I find fewer people can use angle rods. This suggests that a different degree of sensitivity is required for angle rods and my recent experience confirms this. When the angle rods would no longer work for me I found that I could still use the vee rod all day without any exhaustion of my sensitivity taking place.

A request had been made to the Society for the assistance of a dowser to locate a culvert which was known to be buried at a depth of about 20ft. in playing fields adjacent to a school. Extentions to the school were in course of construction and it was hoped to use the culvert to carry the rainwater away from the roofs.

The exact position of the culvert was not known and to excavate a trench 20ft. deep across the side would have been an expensive operation. Many years ago a small stream ran across the site and when tipping was about to take place the stream was piped in. When tipping was completed the playing fields were made and in one of these was a large underground chamber into which the culvert discharged, this was to be the starting point of the survey.

Before making a start it is necessary to look round about to see whether there is anything which may cause a false diagnosis to be made.

Overhead cables may cause rod reaction should any be in the vicinity but a short bar of material placed in the lapel of the jacket, horizontally, will prevent this when using angle rods but the bar should be vertical when using a vee rod. When very sensitive angle rods are being used they can be affected when passing between two trees, shrubs or plants of the same species and it may be necessary to use samples in an opposing manner to prevent this happening.

There are several ways in which the course of a drain, water pipe or cable may be followed, each having its own particular advantage. Providing it is not very windy the easiest and certainly the quickest way is to use angle rods.

When following the course of a drain or pipe the way the rods turn varies according to the polarity of the body of the operator.

The rods will either turn inwards forming a cross (x) or will turn outwards forming a vee (v). The majority of operators will find the rods turn inwards. When the operator is walking immediately above the pipe the X (or V) will be symmetrical but should he wander off course a little the X (or V) will become deformed and a change of direction is indicated.

It is advisable to stop at intervals, lower the forearms to re-align the rods, and then raise the rods and re-commence walking. The rods will once more form the X (or V) should the pipe still be underfoot.

One advantage of this method is that branches are easily found, one of the rods will turn when this occurs. When a branch is found on the left hand side the right hand rod will turn (X operator) and when the branch is on the right the left hand rod will turn. The opposite occurs when the operator is of the V class. Incidentally, this provides a good way to find the position of a blockage in a drain. As an approach is made along the course of the drain the rods will turn partly, forming an X (or V) and when the position of the blockage is reached the rods will complete the turn.

Leakages from a water pipe or drain can also be found in this manner. The way the rods turn may sometimes reverse when following the course of a pipe in which the water is flowing. When the operator is following the course of the pipe against the flow of water the rods may turn outwards where previously walking with the flow they turned inwards, this is a useful method to find out which way water is flowing and provides another easy way to find the position of a leakage. The similarity will be seen here with the way a vee rod behaves when walking with the flow or against it.

Angle rods commence turning at a greater distance from the object than its depth below ground level, until, when, immediately over the object, they will have turned so far that one rod will be immediately over the other, because of this the 45 degree parallels are not found with angle rods and other means have to be used to find the depth of an object.

For the benefit of the uninitiated the 45 degree parallels are positions on each side of a buried object where vee rod reaction occurs and their distance from a position immediately above the object is equal to the depth of the object below ground level. There are other parallels further out but these give a much weaker reaction and if you do not think about them they will not trouble you. This method of finding depth is known as the Bishop's Rule and it is very accurate.

To use angle rods for finding depth the rods must first be calibrated. By experiment the place at which to make marks on the rods can be found so that as a buried object is being approached the position will be reached where one mark is over the other at a distance from the object equal to its depth. Confusion sometimes arises between the location of the parallels and the actual object but this can be avoided.

The vee rod reacts when the edges of the object are passed over, first from one side and then from the other but when a 45 degree parallel is passed over rod reaction only occurs when the parallel is passed over walking away from the object and not when walking towards it, other dowsers find this to be so. When the rod reacts in a certain place therefore all that is required to find out whether a parallel has been located or the edge of an object is to turn and walk over the position from the opposite direction, should the rod turn again it will be known that an object has been located, if it does not turn it will be a parallel that has been found.

To avoid being diverted by other pipes or cables, etc., which may be in the vicinity a sufficiently comprehensive selection of samples should be used in an opposing manner so that the angle rods will not be affected when walking over objects in which there is no interest. Samples of material of which the pipe and contents to be located are composed are not of course included.

When opposing samples are being used it will be found that the rods become more sensitive, fields from many objects surround us and although these may not cause rod reaction they do appear to restrain rod movement.

When a sample is held *upright in the right hand* with the short limb of the angle rod it will oppose the field from an object of the same composition and prevent the rods from turning. Several samples may be placed in a container which itself must be elongated. A container may be secured to the top of the short limb.

When eliminating samples are not in use the edges of an object are located but when an elongated sample is held *upright in the left hand* it acts as an intensifier and the rods will turn whenever material similar to the sample is underfoot, try walking on a lawn with a piece of grass as a sample, you should not be able to walk more than a few paces before the rods close.

Should a strong wind be blowing the vee rod may be used instead of the angle rods to follow the course of a pipe but this takes longer, the 45 degree parallels are found and must be identified.

Mr. Thompson's double vee rod is very useful for following the course of a pipe, one can proceed along over the pipe in a zig-zag manner, the rod flicking over as the pipe is crossed first from one side then from the other. When carrying out this particular survey I used a vee rod to follow the course of the culvert.

Following an operation my dowsing sensitivity, only so far as angle rods were concerned, used to be very quickly exhausted and I could only make about six locations with them in one day, I had therefore to be careful and not waste any of my precious six but use a vee rod wherever possible and reserve the use of the angle rod for determining the composition and size of the located objects.

It is my belief that the electrical activity of the brain is the source of our dowsing sensitivity and so I had no hesitation in asking my doctor if he would arrange for an E.E.G. to be made, I was confident that some defect would be shewn and such was the case. The E.E.G., which was made at the electrical physiology department of a large hospital, shewed that the electrical activity was low on the right hand side of my brain but X-rays and the pretty pictures made on the brain scanner shewed that there was no structure defect in the brain. I should like to tell you more about this experience later on if there is time but for the moment suffice to say that after over two and a half years of this rapid exhaustion of my angle rod sensitivity I am extremely grateful to our Radionic Practitioner member Miss E. Grindley, A.R.I.B.A., who carried out an investigation into my condition and came up with the answer. After the Black Box treatment Miss Grindley gave me my capability gradually increased, over a period of five days, until I had fully recovered my sensitivity. I can now use my angle rods all day long, on the fifth day I made sixty locations without exhausting my sensitivity and only gave up then because I was tired with walking about so much.

It was interesting to hear from the consultant that in his opinion dowsing was due to what he called Electrical projection from the body.

Following the treatment given to me by Miss Grindley, another E.E.G. was made and this was now found to be normal, the electrical activity on the right hand side of the brain was much stronger.

Reverting to the culvert, I located it every 10 yards or so as I proceeded across the fields, the builders foreman placing pegs at the positions where rod reaction occurred.

Usually I use white plastic tumblers filled with cement mortar as markers as these can easily be seen and placed.

Gradually the pegs could be seen to be forming a straight line until suddenly we moved off at a tangent and another line of pegs developed.

When the school boundary was reached I used my angle rods to find the size of the drain and to make an analysis of its composition and found that what I had latterly been following was a six inch salt glazed drain pipe and this was not of sufficient size for the purpose.

The method used to find the size of the drain is quite simple once the basic principles are understood.

Firstly, the strength of the field from an object increases in direct proportion to the increase in the thickness of the object. This can be demonstrated by using an angle rod fitted with a variable damper which, when applied, restrains progressively the free turning movement of the rods. The amount of tension applied to the damper is registered by a pointer on a dial, the position at which the damper just touches the rod is our zero.

(Such a device is incorporated in a patent I have recently been granted for an improved form of angle rod).

An object of known thickness is passed over several times and the pressure on the damper is increased each time until finally the rods turn about one inch and then stop. The number of degrees the pointer has turned on the dial is noted and the damper is left applied.

An object of the same thickness as the first object is placed on top of the latter and the procedure is repeated, it will be found that the reading for the two objects is about twice that when only one object was passed over. Secondly, as an approach is being made towards a buried pipe the angle through which the rods turn varies, at a given distance from the pipe, according to the diameter of the pipe, the angle becomes greater as the diameter of the pipe increases.

By experiment marks are made on the rods, where one crosses the other, relative to pipes of various sizes.

The rods must not be too free and the speed of approach must be a little slower than usual and consistent.

When using angle rods the state of mind of the operator is even more important than when using a vee rod, he must be completely relaxed and detached and must not think deeply about anything. I find that should anything disturb me I may not get a rod reaction in a place where only a few seconds before I got a strong reaction, also he should not talk.

There are many similarities between the changes that take place, in some circumstances, in the electrical activity of the brain and in the performance of dowsing.

Another thing which may mystify a physical dowser is that usually, when using angle rods the eyes must be focused on the rods, should the eyes be raised the rods may not turn, there is nothing occult about this however. A circular disc can be fixed to the person, on the lapel of the jacket preferably, when the eyes may be raised. The disc is beamed to the far end of the rods. The most suitable length for angle rods is 18 inches and the reaction is stronger when the ends of the rods are looked at. The lighter the rods are, without diminishing the cross sectional area and the more certain is the reaction but heavier rods are required when it is windy, when operating outdoors. As with a vee rod there is usually a slight kick in the opposite direction to which the rods will finally turn when the object has been located. Reverting again to the culvert, we have so far found the position of a drain which is not large enough for the purpose and so back again to the position where we branched off at a tangent on the first line of pegs. It was found that what we had latterly been following was a branch that the main culvert carried on in a straight line.

The course of the culvert was followed until the school boundary was reached, a peg was placed above the culvert in a convenient position for ultimate excavation. Making use of The Bishop's Rule the depth of the culvert was found and with the use of angle rods the size and composition was determined.

I cannot find a sure way of finding out the composition of an object when using a vee rod in conjunction with samples but I find the use of material samples with angle rods to be extremely accurate.

Before any attempt can be made at an analysis a sufficient number of opposing samples must be used in order that when the object is passed by, or walked over, no movement of the rods occurs, this is the basis of my practice and it is very simple.

When a sample is removed from this number the rods will turn when similar material is present in the object. To continue the analysis the removed sample should be replaced and another sample removed, by a process of elimination it will soon be found out of what the object is composed.

As the angle rods are made more sensitive when holding a number of samples the number of materials which can cause rod reaction increases, particularly lightweight materials and smaller objects will be found. Distant prospection will also be found to be greatly improved.

An opposing sample is one that is of elongated form held upright in the *right hand* but a smaller irregular shaped sample placed in an elongated container which will then act in the same manner, when correctly held.

While the sample held in the *left hand* acts as an intensifier and causes the angle rods to turn when over a large area of alien material, not only when passing over the edges, it is of great assistance in locating objects which are very small and which, without this sample, would not cause rod reaction. A container filled with water is very effective in finding very small underground water flows but it is of no use when the ground is wet, the rods will turn every few paces, the water on the ground itself will cause rod reaction. When an intensifying sample is being used opposing samples of materials in which there is no interest must be used to prevent the rods from being influenced by objects of such materials which may be encountered. A container filled with coal gas can be used to determine whether a pipe contains gas, opposing samples of iron and possibly carbon being used to cancel out the pipe and a container of water to cancel out water.

Angle rods have one great failing unless you know how to overcome it. They are very susceptible to picking up stray fields, rays of union, witness rays, ghosts or images you will hear them called.

When an object on one side of the operator is passed one rod will turn and point to the object. When an object is passed on the other side of the operator the other rod will turn. It will be seen that when there are two objects, one on each side of the operator both rods will turn, each pointing to an object. The rods will now be in the position they occupy when an object has been located underfoot but excavation would reveal that no alien object was there. The vee rod is not affected in this manner but the pendulum can be. What is in effect a magnetic screen or shield may be laid on the ground to prevent the rods from being influenced in this manner.

A continuous length of any kind of material will serve, say a length of half inch plastic hose pipe joined together by means of a short piece of wood dowel. This is laid to form a path in which to operate and when walking within this only objects on or in the ground will cause the rods to completely turn when an object is located. The rods will partly turn when an object outside the shield is passed nearby. A sample of the material of which the shield is composed must be used to oppose the field from the shield itself otherwise the rods would turn continually as the operator walked about within the shield.

This failing of the angle rods however can be made use of with advantage. An object may be placed on the ground as a witness and should another object of the same composition be in the vicinity the resulting ray of union can easily be followed, and the hidden object located.

I heard nothing from the architect until a year to the day when I received a letter from him asking me to ring him with a view to making arrangements to visit another school where they wanted me to locate another culvert for them. I asked how they had got on at the other site and he said " Oh yes, it was there under your peg." " What about the depth I asked? " " It was within a few inches of the depth you gave," he replied, which was I believe, given as approximately 18ft. 6in. And the size I asked? " Well that was rather funny, he replied, when my clerk of works rang me up to tell me that they had found the culvert he said " It is not 15in. though, it is only 12in., and we have broken it," but when I visited the site in the afternoon I went down the ladder and taking out my rule I found that it was a 15in. pipe after all."

I rather suspect though that the men carrying out the excavation had little faith that the culvert would be below them otherwise they would have used more care when they were approaching the given depth.

OLD MINEWORKING INVESTIGATION
H. Guttridge

Some time ago I was asked, by a firm of structural engineers, to assist in carrying out an investigation into the extent and nature of some old ironstone workings at Lincoln, where mining had been carried out over 100 years ago.

As often happens, accurate records were not available and the extent of the workings was not known, nor was it known whether the overburden had settled. It was known, however, that the ironstone had been extracted using the pillar and stall method of mining.

The ironstone had outcropped and that was where the mining had been started. The pillars left to support the roof, while mining is in progress, may be continuous or isolated. When the miners have gone as far as desired, the pillars are removed as the miners withdraw, allowing the roof to settle.

It occurred to me that if that was the case there may have been cavities left on the perimeter of the workings and that I should look for these first.

When searching for voids I use, first of all, a special type of angle rod, so designed and constructed that the rods will only turn when passing over or by voids. They will not turn when passing over any alien object in the ground which may be encountered. This saves a lot of time, particularly when dowsing in built-up areas, where so many pipes, cables, drains, conduits, etc., may be otherwise located. I do not believe in doing anything the hard way ; if an easier, quicker and more certain way is available I always use it.

We arrived at the site just before lunch and I prospected with the special angle rods, down a footpath leading from the road. After walking about 20 yards both rods turned, very decisively, indicating that the edge of a void had been passed over.

I always immediately verify angle rod findings with a small whalebone Vee rod. The Vee rod enables the position to be marked with great accuracy and is unaffected by stray fields, which angle rods are particularly susceptible to. Another reason why I always use a Vee rod, when possible, is that, unlike angle rods, I do not find using a Vee rod at all exhausting. Angle rods should not be used more than is necessary.

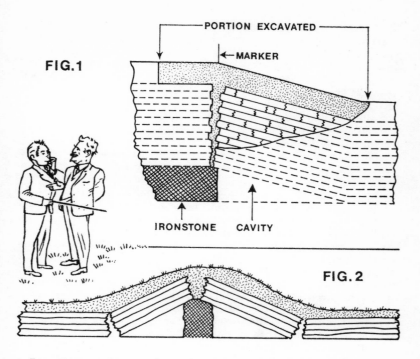

FIG.1

PORTION EXCAVATED

MARKER

IRONSTONE   CAVITY

FIG.2

Location confirmed, I marked the position and by means of Bishop's Rule and Vee rod found that the depth of my location was 14ft. 6in. below ground level.

I moved further away and made other approaches and locations, at intervals, until I had plotted the extent of the workings along one side of the site.

It had been arranged that an excavator should be on site after lunch and the machine was set to work on one of the positions I had marked. At a depth of about 3ft. hard limestone rock was encountered and the bottom of the trench was cleaned up. It was seen that at the position I had marked was a gap in the limestone about 15in. wide, filled with brown soil.

It is always a moment of great satisfaction to me to excavate at the time and see then and there what my dowsing has located. I shall never forget an incident which took place at a school in Lancashire where I was to locate a concrete culvert. As a preliminary I followed some drains from tennis court gullies, which all led to one position in a lawn, but there was nothing visible on the surface. I diagnosed that there was either a manole or a catchpit at that point, a marker was placed at each corner.

The Headmaster had asked if a class of boys could watch my activities, and they with the Head were all standing nearby. I carefully positioned the excavator and the driver forced the bucket into the soft lawn exactly where I indicated. The bucket entered the ground to a depth of about 18in., and, drawing the bucket towards the machine, he slowly raised it up. The Oohs and Ahs from the boys had to be heard to be believed, as the bucket came up and brought with it one edge of a large stone slab covering a catchpit. Lumps of soil falling into the water further heightened the drama of the moment. The Headmaster rushed up to me and, placing his hands on my shoulders, said, " I should never have believed it had I not seen it with my own eyes."

But I digress.

On one side of the soil-filled fissure in the rock at the bottom of the trench the rock was seen to be smooth and unbroken, while on the other side the rock was fractured. This was fortunate, as it allowed the machine to excavate, although not without difficulty. As excavation proceeded it was observed that the fissure was getting narrower and that it was still filled with soil which had worked down over the years. The strata of the limestone could be plainly seen on the excavated trench side and took a decided slant downwards (see Fig. 2). After excavating about 9ft., digging became difficult. The machine was about at its limit for depth and also sufficient time had been spent on this one trial hole. A 4ft. crowbar could be fully inserted into the fissure and if let go would have dropped out of sight.

It is often tantalising to get so near an objective when carrying out excavations and then have to stop for one reason or another. In this case it would have meant bringing a larger machine to the site. This would have been expensive and would not have added materially to our knowledge, but I wish we had been able to remove the remaining 3ft. or so and expose the cavity, as a matter of interest.

Our excavation had proved to our satisfaction that we were on the boundary of the mine workings. Another marked position was excavated down to limestone and again the soil-filled fissure was found. In one case the fissure was about 2ft. away from the marked position ; the rock had apparently not broken immediately above the edge of the cavity. The site was of considerable extent and in the remaining time available I made a survey of the area, trying to find any further voids.

The special angle rods will locate isolated voids from a considerable distance. One rod will turn when a void has been located and indicate the change of direction required to lead one to it. Wherever I walked on the site one rod turned towards the centre, where there was a mound. All the way round the mound my rods indicated a void and with a Vee rod I plotted the extent ; it was almost circular. This led to the conclusion that an isolated pillar had not been removed for some reason. It was not possible to excavate, as the mound was in the middle of a cultivated allotment. Little did the long-dead miners think that I should stand there one day, being curious about their work.

A PRACTICAL WATER DIVINER SPEAKS
George Applegate

I should like to begin by telling you how I first became interested in water divining. It was introduced to me at quite an early age and in a rather strange way. I was serving my apprenticeship with a company that specialised in putting heating installations into very large country houses. My father was the Chief Engineer of G. N. Hayden & Sons, who then had their head office in Trowbridge. They have now become a nationwide organisation.

We were working at a very large country house, The Grange, at Edington. The owner was spending a fortune on his property, but the last thing he had thought about was getting water. He had a well-known contractor there, who put down 6 boreholes. They were all abortive and, of course, he was getting quite frantic and we were laughing at his misfortune, poor man. One day a gentleman arrived who was going to put an end to all his troubles. That was Mr. Joe Mullins of Bath. He picked a site exactly between 2 existing boreholes, and all of you know the reason why. But he happened to put the bore down on the right spot. He worked on the terms of " no water no pay" and his borehole was highly successful. Having an inquisitive mind, I wanted to know why he had succeeded when everybody else had failed, and my father explained that he was a very well-known water diviner. I imitated his actions and found that I, too, got quite a strong reaction over this particular spot, but I got reactions everywhere else in the district as well, so I knew even at that early age that there was something more to water divining than catching hold of a twig and getting a lot of reactions.

From that day onwards the subject of dowsing took up a great deal of my spare time. I got the cold shoulder from most professional dowsers. They just didn't want to share my enthusiasm and I think it was sheer persistence, nothing else, that enabled me to continue and eventually become a successful dowser. I owe a great debt of gratitude to some of the founder members of this Society.

Captain Trinder, who was a nearby neighbour, was helpful, and Major Pogson, whom I worked with on many projects, I found to be a tower of strength in my hour of need. I think it is true to say one learns more from one's disappointments and failures than from one's successes, but I wanted to cut my failures to the very minimum, so I tried to find out why so many other people had failed on particular sites. I produced data on some thousand boreholes that were not regarded as fully successful and I received co-operation from many of the leading companies in this country.

My success came as a result of the prompting of a well-known geologist, Mr. Whitfield, who was employed by the Ministry to find water over a large area. He had investigated the subject of water divining and had chosen a site for a regional scheme at Mere in West Wiltshire. It was a geologically perfect site, but he realised that if the site was going to be 100% successful he would need the help of somebody else in siting the bore. We came to terms on the basis that 2 boreholes should be put down; he would site one and would allow me to site the other. This was the answer to a water diviner's dream. I undertook this job at quite a tender age and it was very successful. My borehole, which was the shallower of the two, produced 3 times more water than Mr. Whitfield's. To this day they are extracting 2 million gallons a day from this borehole and it is, of course, quite a major scheme. Further boreholes have been put down in the area and at the opening of these boreholes I was introduced to the then Under-Secretary at the Ministry of Health. It was Mr. Enoch Powell, so I had the privilege of meeting this gentleman at a very early age, when he was at the beginning of his political career.

Soon I was being employed by farmers and small well-boring contractors to locate water supplies for farms. Usually the farmers were so short of water that if the borehole produced 500 gallons a day they thought they were in heaven. One could hardly fail with such small quantities and everybody was happy provided he had some water. But for me this wasn't very rewarding and I branched out into larger fields, purely on the basis of trying to get data together. I realised that if I was going to follow this interest through to a satisfactory conclusion as an engineer I had to tackle it in a practical manner. This was somewhat frustrating to some of my colleagues, who were going off on entirely the opposite tack. It is only fair to say that I have now completed the circle and come back to the point where I began. I don't necessarily feel that I have achieved very much scientifically other than the fact that I know I can find water.

Some of the larger jobs I did were for breweries, to whom water, or liquor as they call it, is their life blood. I received an urgent call one day from Whitbreads the brewers to go to their Stroud brewery, where the water supply had suddenly stopped. This frequently happens but, of course, there was some geological reason for it.   I carried out an extensive investigation around the area and at the immediate site and found that their water supply had, in fact, dried up.   They were therefore faced with the problem of either getting a new source or closing down the brewery, and, having recently spent a considerable sum of money on modernisation, with new bottling plant, they were most anxious to develop the brewery.   The local water board were unable to meet their commitments in the town and rural areas, let alone supply industry with any increased quantity, so permission was given for trial boreholes to be put down at sites that I selected.   Geologically it was a difficult site, as the Stroud Valley is a complex one, although it may look straightforward on a geological map.   I picked what was regarded by many people, including those who examined the area, as a most unacceptable site from most points of view. It was difficult to get the well-boring equipment in there, it was difficult to pipe up to, in fact, there was very little to commend it except that I knew there was water there, and they were willing to take my word for it.   Fortunately, the bores proved successful and the water was duly piped up to the brewery, which was kept going.   Whitbreads were very grateful.   I had a letter from Colonel Whitbread and I have done several jobs for them since. I was greatly relieved that my name didn't even creep into your Journal at that time, because I had my picture on the front page of the local paper.   I felt some embarrassment, because I was in my early days as a water diviner and, having had 2 failures, had sworn to myself that I would not publicise my work until I had had 100 successes.   But, of course, when I had had 100 successes I was too busy even to talk about it.

One Sunday I went by helicopter, picked up by Billy Butlin from the local football pitch, to Minehead Holiday Camp, which he had just opened.   He had a camp full of people and no water coming out of the end of the pipe, so the position was desperate. Everybody had said there was no water in the district.   Well, we all know that there is water in almost every district, but sometimes it is geologically difficult to get at and on the coast one was likely to get saline inflows from the sea.   Basically there wasn't very much to commend the site and I realised the whole job was going to be complex, bearing in mind the vast water requirements. A holiday camp is equal to a town, and with its peak demands for hot water, for swimming pools, kitchens and laundry the water requirements were in excess of a million gallons a day.   Mr. Butlin was faced with the problem of either cancelling all the bookings, with a considerable loss of revenue, or of bringing in water by ship or by tanker; he was considering every feasible possibility.

I found there were 7 underground streams converging on the camp like the spokes of a wheel.   It was almost like a miracle and I was able to trace these right up into the hills many miles away. Boreholes were put down; I only called for shallow bores because of the problem of the saline inflow. At 70 feet the first borehole hit 23,000 gallons an hour, and so on. In the end we had nearly 2 million gallons a day being pumped out of Butlin's Holiday Camp. This water supply is now being used by the North Somerset Water Board and is one of their major sources, so Butlin is now making money out of his borehole, whereas at the time he was considering having to close the camp.

Needless to say, I have done quite a lot of jobs for Butlin's Holiday Camps since that one, but the thing which really impressed me was that the well-boring contractors turned up within 24 hours with big well-boring equipment, and within a week pumps were installed and the water was coming out of the ground. The incredible thing wasn't finding the water—probably many of our members could have gone to the site and found water—but the fact that it was being pumped out of the ground in such a short time. I don't think it would be possible to do that today; the opening of that camp took place some years ago.

Water boards usually spend a lot of money and end up with a dry borehole. Then they may call me in in desperation. But I should like to tell you about one or two jobs I have done for water boards where large quantities of water were involved. For the Shropshire Water Board I found in excess of 2 million gallons a day, North Cotswold the same amount; Dorset Water Board, and so on and so forth. I think the classic example of a muddled situation was a job that I did for the Portland Cement Company, when they built a cement factory and found that their water supply had dried up and was almost non-existent. I think Miss Bent and I spent a lot of time on that one. But it is quite incredible to me that people will leave the question of the water supply until almost the last minute and then call in the dowser in complete desperation.

One situation I tackled had a funny side to it. I was dowsing at Axbridge right up on the top of the Mendips. I am very fond of the countryside and I dress up in an old pair of breeches and an old tweed jacket, and I suppose I look pretty rough when I am out walking around in the fields. I am sure I must, because on this occasion it had a sequel. I was walking down a little gully when suddenly I was pounced upon and held down on the ground by 2 very strong men. I kicked myself clear and hit one of them. I must have caught him just right, because he was quite dazed for a while. Then I was arrested by the other man, who turned out to be a policeman. In due course I was charged at Axbridge Police Station with being a poacher. They said they had been after me for about 3 weeks. They were so pleased they had caught me, and it wasn't until the Clerk of the Water Board came out and identified me that I was released. Needless to say, I wasted a lot of time, but I received an apology in due course and look back on the whole thing with a little bit of amusement. But a similar incident in Spain was much more unpleasant. I was arrested by the Spanish police for being a smuggler when I was doing a job in the Pyrenees. So one incurs a certain risk when going round the countryside, and I think the B.S.D. should provide us with membership cards or something similar to enable us to identify ourselves.

To come a little nearer home, if one tries to keep one's feet on the ground the day to day status of a water diviner is a lot easier than when I started. I find that I am now readily accepted wherever I go; the whole professional attitude towards a water diviner has changed in the last 20 years. That brings me to the thought of what does the future hold and how is it going to be moulded, so that future water diviners can be correctly trained to enable them to play an important part, especially in arid countries, where water is a vital necessity. In this country we are blessed with a water supply system which provides us with practically all the water we need, although it is doubtful whether it will be able to keep pace with the present extravagant requirements. But developing countries need our assistance more than ever, and my calls are frequently to countries where they need water and cannot develop in any way until they get it. My travels take me to the 4 corners of the earth. A fortnight ago I was in Calgary, Alberta. A few weeks before that I was sniffing over the top of a borehole a few miles from Pittsburg. One has to be prepared to travel and I always work on the basis of "no success no pay," so I cannot afford to be too wrong if perhaps £500 worth of expenses have accrued to me before I start.

There is a world shortage of qualified water diviners and I think the B.S.D. has an important function to play in training and stimulating the interest of people who would be willing to work hard and become practising water diviners. I realise as much as anybody that the old methods of training, of passing on by word of mouth, of developing one's own system are not going to be acceptable in this changing modern world, and I feel that our Society can play an important part in training the younger generation. I have been able to develop a system and to train water diviners. I have had Australians come to me for training and Indians and people from other developing countries. One *can* train a water diviner who has a natural gift to become a professional in a comparatively short time. Having had such a struggle myself, having had the cold shoulder from so many practising water diviners who were somewhat jealous of their professional art, I feel it is **my** duty to encourage and help the young enthusiast as much as possible.

I would like to tell you about a simple but very interesting job that I undertook a few weeks ago. It was on a site for the Continental Oil Company—Conoco. They are the owners of the Jet Petrol Company and they have a very large oil terminal near Sheffield. This consists of what they call a tank farm, huge underground petrol tanks and oil tanks connected to a central oil line which pumps up from the coast. They were getting a discharge of diesel oil into the river, which was killing all the trout. It was a case of pollution and the local authority were making an order to close the depot under the new Act. They flew me up to Manchester, picked me up by car and took me over to the site. They were desperate, because they had brought in a contractor and the whole place was in a state of chaos. There were holes you could sink a large building into, bulldozers all over the place and gangs of men. The wages bill was £1,000 a day for the men on the site trying to find the leak.

To be quite honest, until I reached the site I didn't know how I was going to tackle the job. I realised it was a very complex site with pipe-lines all over the place, but going along in the plane I suddenly thought, "What I have got to do is sort out all the things I *can* identify before I start to look for the leak." In so doing I found 3 very deep-seated flows of water and I traced with the Engineer most of the oil lines and the pipe-lines. Then, having sorted out all the things that I could readily identify, I started to look for the flow of oil that was coming from somewhere and getting into the river. Thanks to a certain amount of good luck, I found a reaction running right through the depot. Fortunately it ran right underneath the centre of one of their excavations. Using my own method, I took a depth reading on the flow and found that they had to go just 2 feet deeper to find out what was there. I persuaded the contractor, a very large firm from Rotherham, to concentrate on this hole while I was there and scoop it out 2 feet. You have to bear in mind that there were 20 or 30 deep holes all round the site that were bone dry, but when he just pulled out the 2 feet I was pleased to see the oil bubbling up through the ground. The flow of oil was now found, and we traced it back to a pressure line which had a very small hole in it, and, of course, it didn't take too long to fix that.

The interesting thing about this site from the purely engineering point of view was how to stop contamination from the huge area of saturated oil. A channel was dug across the site and they are still pumping out seepage oil today, but it is now seeping into this large hole instead of into the river. That is a practical application dealing with an entirely different subject, but one from which I gained a considerable amount of useful experience.

A water diviner is faced with a problem. He feels an inner glow of satisfaction when he is successful, but success is strong wine and one has to be cautious. One has to think the problem out and I spend a great deal of time in research before I go to a site. I do this because I suppose by nature I am somewhat lazy, and I figure that if I can sort things out from paper, maps, geological reports, it will save a lot of time and trouble. I find this really does pay off. The successes one has prompt one to carry on, although I should be quite happy to pack this job up. I find it is taking up too much of my time and I am spending too much time away from my home. I only wish to goodness there was someone who could step into my shoes and take some of the jobs off my shoulders. A problem I find today is one whereby you act in arbitrations sometimes between the owner, the unsuccessful borehole driller, maybe a local authority, and sometimes you end up in Court giving evidence, and this may waste days. One doesn't know today who is controlling the water in this country, whether it is the Water Boards, the River Boards or the Ministry. It is complete chaos, and some new legislation has to be forthcoming if our underground sources of water are to be exploited properly, so that areas are not completely dried up, and sources of water which at the moment are running to waste can be used.

I think one of the most rewarding jobs I ever did was on a little farm near Sherborne in Dorset, where a very young farmer and his wife had taken a small-holding. I suppose the only reason they had got this small-holding at a low price was that there was no water supply on it. He was a hard-working man but had got himself into financial difficulties. He had no water and he had to have it. A well-boring contractor called me in and said, " It doesn't look as if we'll ever get paid for the job, but if you are willing to help this man so are we." I found out that just on the corner of the site in an area of 9 feet there was an underground spring of water. It cut across his corner between 2 other people's properties but it was just within his boundary. I think everybody else who had looked at the site must have missed that little corner, because 3 other diviners had surveyed it and told him there was no water available. When the borehole was put down it was the only really good artesian bore that I have ever hit, because it came up 12 feet in the air and the water was as pure as gin. It was the most perfect sample of water that I have ever seen. Realising the value that had been put on that man's farm gave me more personal satisfaction than to find a million gallons a day for a water board. Today he owns the two adjoining farms and I like to think that his success somehow sprang from my success in finding that particular site.

DOCKS AND DOWSING

E.K. Whittle

It has been said that man began to use technology without knowing exactly what it was. That is how I started dowsing. I had been using it and not realising it. My experience goes back not only to docks but to the railways in the age of steam.

I started work for the London and North Eastern Railway Company in 1939, when I was about 25 years of age. I had served my time as a fitter and when I came out of my time I went to sea as a junior marine engineer. After 2 years, which covered 3 voyages, the ship came in for repair. In those days I think you got a day's leave for each month you spent at sea. Well, the last voyage was 9 months, so I got 9 days' leave. After that I was on my own, receiving no payment, so I went to the Labour Exchange and they told me that the railway wanted a mechanical fitter. It was to have been a stopgap job until the shipping company sent for me, but I found the work so interesting that I stayed with the railway company, who also owned the Hull docks system, until October, 1976, when I took early retirement after 37½ years' service.

My first work was with what was known as the Outside Machinery Department, who used to be called upon to work anywhere on the rail system. This covered the 7 miles of docks (at the time) and the rail routes in and out of Hull for quite a distance, the rail depots, pumping stations, etc., but not the motive power units, i.e. railway engines and rolling stock. In those days there were a vast number of steam prime movers, most important among them being railside pumping stations to supply water to supply tanks, from which the steam locomotives took their water supply. We had a problem at one of the pumping stations, miles from anywhere, on the Hull to Barnsley rail link, a very important South Yorkshire delivery route for the coal trains to Hull's Alexandra Dock. This dock was the main outlet from which coal was shipped all over the world.

The practice was that if you were strange to the work, as I was, you were put to work with somebody older than yourself, and I was sent out with an old fitter called Chris. He was a strange chap but with a wonderful knowledge of steam engines, and he used to keep ferrets. It was said that he kept one in his pocket during the war when there was a cigarette famine. At this distance of time it seems hard to believe, but cigarettes really were very, very scarce, and he felt that when he took his coat off somebody might be tempted to put his hand in his pocket to see if he had left any cigarettes in it. That was when his little friend made himself useful.

Chris carried a tool bag, because we sometimes used a hammer or chisel—you don't get so much of that nowadays—and when he packed his tools he always took with him two pieces of galvanised wire about 18in. long bent at right angles to 6in. long. I said, " What do you use these for? " and he said, " They might come in useful."

This pumping station had a supply well some distance behind it and the usual two locomotive boilers and two steam pumps to supply a large water tank on legs for the use of thirsty locomotives. We were told on arrival that the pumps were working but not delivering water, which indicated a blown flange joint. No one seemed to know where the pipe ran from the well to the pumping station and the land was covered with scrub, etc. That was where the old fitter's two pieces of wire came in. He took them out and held them chest high, and as they crossed he tracked over the covered pipe, marking out its route. Knowing that the pipe was in regular lengths, it was only a question of time before the faulty joint was found. Considering that the pipe was buried about 2ft. down, to be out of the way of frost damage, to find and repair the fault with the aid of two little ¼in. galvanised rods seemed like magic to me. He didn't call it dowsing, just pipe finding. He said, " Keep it to yourself, lad." I tried it and after a bit of practice found that I could do it quite well and took his hint to keep it to myself. Later on I found that quite a lot of the older fitters and some of the plumbers could use angle rods, mostly as a short cut in work practice on water pipes, nothing else. Nobody thought much about it. It was just something that we could do, like riding a bicycle. As to using the rods to find water, it never entered our heads.

After the war years the coal trade fell away, the coal hoists were taken down and, as we all know, diesel power took over from steam. Maybe it was a mistake, with the discovery of the massive deposits to be mined at Selby, but the Hull-Barnsley rail link is no more. As the dock system contracted with the larger ships now in use the smaller docks, mid-Victorian Albert Dock, Victoria Dock, etc., were being reorganised and the old D.C. electrical system was being taken up and replaced by A.C. equipment. About 1950 the railways were nationalised and the docks were taken under the (as now) British Transport Docks Board. I was asked which I would rather be with, British Rail or Docks Maintenance. I said yes to the docks, because I lived near them. I thus came in contact with the Electrical Dept. and noticed that some of their senior electrical engineers were using, and showing the junior electrical engineers how to use, angle rods to locate old electric cables. These are quite valuable for scrap and thousands of pounds' worth were found by that method. In the heavy damage which Hull received in the last war the plans had been lost, so nobody had any idea where anything was.

I was quite intrigued by this use of angle rods. There were many arguments as to the whys and wherefores, but I don't think the electrical engineers realised that the rods could be used to find water and we didn't know that they would find electric cables. The size of rods and the materials seemed to vary but the results were the same. One thing seemed certain—some were better at using them than others. The electricians' knowledge came from highly technical sources, whereas we were very practical people. No one as yet called it dowsing.

An article in a magazine on dowsing triggered me off to find out more about this business. I cut myself a V rod out of a hazel bush and was very surprised when I got a reaction on the old " Citadel " site on Victoria Dock, which is part of Hull old town.

In 1970, when we were building an absolutely up-to-date workshop costing half a million pounds, which was to be devoted to the repair of diesel appliances among other work, I didn't do any pipe finding then, it wasn't necessary, but rods were still being used to find electrical cables on the dock. Some of the young apprentices said to me, " Can you do this? " I said, " Of course I can, I used to do it years ago." I showed them how to use the rods and they went marching off to find water. Now a friend of mine had been using the rods to find water but had not detected electrical cables. " You wouldn't," I told him. " It depends on what your mind is on. If you are looking for water pipes you won't find electric cables and vice versa." That gave him something to think about.

One day a man came with a tape recorder to see " the chap who could find water with a rod." I had no option but to show him and it was put out next morning on our local radio station, Humberside Radio. On two occasions I gave them demonstrations, going over old pipes, drains, etc. I no longer minded people being present when I was working with V rods or angle rods. I also tried hawthorn rods. They seemed a but prickly at first and I felt a bit strange using them on the dock, but I soon got the hang of them. I wanted to go further into the subject and find out something about the other properties that dowsing covered, so I joined the BSD.

In 1976 I went to the Peebles Congress and there I saw Mrs. Smithett demonstrate map dowsing. It was my first introduction to that subject. I am a practical sort of chap, so I wouldn't like to say what I thought about it. However, I decided to give it a trial and about a week later, when I was back home again, I tried it out on an ordnance map of the Hull district. I made two or three pendulums and I thought, " Here goes." It started oscillating and all of a sudden it took off and I said to myself, " Let's go for a walk." I have pretty good eyesight but I couldn't see the names on the map. I knew it was 5-6 miles from the city centre and going in a westerly direction and that was all I did know. I pointed it with a ball point pen and it was right over the spring of the pumping station, which is the main source of Hull's water supply. It came back again towards the centre of Hull and gave two positive signals, one on Queens Gardens and one on Victoria Dock. This dock is being filled in, but it is too soft to walk on and has started to go again.

Back in the 1830's whaling was a big industry in Hull, and we have a remarkable Whaling and Fisheries Museum, which is situated in the old Dock Office building. Going round the show cases I noticed among the products of whalebone and ivory a set of diviner's V rods and a pendulum, beautifully carved. Nothing daunted, I wrote to Mr. Bradshaw, the Director of the Museum, and asked if he would let me try them out. He agreed and told me to make arrangements with his assistant, Mr. A. Credland. This I did and one sunny but cold January morning we tried them out. The V rods were made out of baleen, the pendulum was about the size of a table tennis ball and turned out of a walrus tusk.

At the rear of the museum is the site of the oldest dock in Hull, going back to the mid 1700's, and part of the old town moat, Hull having been originally a walled city, bounded on the east side by the River Hull and on the south by the Humber, the moat following the wall. The moat later became the basis of two docks, the older being the Queen's Dock and the other the Humber Dock. Now about the early 1930s the Queen's Dock (at the rear of the museum) was filled in to form what is now the Queens Gardens, the city's show place, and that is where Mr. Credland and I tried out the whalebone V rods, which he assured me were a great age. About halfway down the dock site, some 100 yards from the Guildhall (better known as the Town Hall), the V rod gave a very positive signal and I knew that there was quite a spring about 30ft. down. Last summer we nearly lost the valuable Cumberland turf in the Queens Gardens. Well, there should be enough water down in that spring to supply the fountains and the whole garden.

Mr. Credland was startled to see the rod bend and wanted to have a go, but by then quite a crowd had collected and he felt a bit selfconscious, so we made our way back to the museum. There we talked a little bit and I told him about the Society and the last Congress. He took his bits and pieces back and then he said, " Do you want some whalebone? " and he brought me two 3 foot lengths. I made them into rods and I have to say I gave some of them to friends within an hour of making them, but I have had the good sense to keep this one.

My father-in-law, now in his eighties, is an old Railway Docks dredgerman and used to dredge Queen's and Victoria Docks in the twenties. I said to him, " When you were dredging Queen's Dock did you ever see a natural spring bubbling up from the bottom? " He said, " Yes." I said, " Could you show me on this map where it was? " I had made a sketch of the neighbourhood, showing the Dock Office, the Technical School, etc., and he said " It was there," and put his finger on the very spot that I had found with the V rod. He said it came gushing up fresh, through the brackish dock water, and when they were working they would dip a bucket in on the end of a rope and use the water for washing purposes or for making tea, but not as drinking water. The lightermen and bargemen used to do the same thing. They had used it for donkey's years. It was a very old dock. " Not only that," he said, " but there was another one, a big one, in Victoria Dock," and he marked the spot where I had been getting a reaction. " That was the main Baltic timber dock, where they used to bring in the softwood from Scandinavia. The seamen in the old steam vessels knew about this spring and instead of paying money to the Water Board they used to put their pipe in and fill their boiler tanks with water from the spring. It was pure, fresh water and very clean." I thought that was very interesting.

The old dock system, I believe, has many springs under it, and it could be that the old town's water supply from Civil War times came from the source which the Water Department's Spring Head Pumping Station has used for the last 80 years. Many wells have been excavated during recent road works in the old town, all on the line under the old Queen's Dock. It is on record that King Charles I, on being refused permission to enter the city during the Civil War, paid the citizens back by poisoning their water supply!

I should like to end with a dowsing anecdote that concerns a friend of mine, Mr. Whitelock. He is a plumber and works for British Rail. He was called out to a stoppage in a supply pipe that runs from the Hessle Pumping Station and supplies the St. Andrew's Fish Dock at the west end of Hull and quite near to the new Humber Bridge site, where they are building the road sections that will eventually hang from the suspension wires. At about the same time that he arrived on the scene, owing to the urgent need to trace the fault the Yorkshire Water Board engineers also arrived with modern water main fault detector apparatus, but owing to outside electronic interference they could not set it up correctly. Thereupon Mr. Whitelock with his angle rods found the route of the pipe and located the leak, which, as luck would have it, was between two sections of the Humber Bridge road fabrications, and had it repaired.

DOWSING FOR SURVIVAL

John Stiles

There must be some new aspirants to dowsing here who have doubts as to whether they can do it. Let me say right away that if you have the ability to dowse you can do anything with it. It is just a question of being patient and working up to it. Don't try to gallop before you can run.

My first introduction to this art, like everybody's probably, was by accident. During the war I was a member of an organisation run by Dingle Foot and the Economic Warfare Boys and the Cloak and Dagger Brigade. While in service in India I was invited, as it were, to laze under the waving palms, but these, of course, existed behind the Japanese rear. At that time my discipline was to train guerrillas to operate behind the enemy lines. In this process, of course, you learn that if you are in jungle territory, or any other territory for that matter, you have got to survive. We had an old Shan forester Old Bill, who taught us all the tricks of what vines to look for, and how you were going to get something to drink, and how you could tell when you were on the run whether you were going forward or backward. Then one day somebody said to him, "Bill, what happens if we have got no vines?" And he said, "Somebody would have to know how to use a twig." Well, the only person in that party at that time who could use a twig was myself. They did all sorts of things to confuse me—towels over my head and buckets of water—but nothing deflected me. When I wanted to find water I found it. I could depth it and when they dug there was the water.

Well, post-war I went in for agriculture and civil engineering. I am an agent general foreman and clerk of works in civil engineering and building construction and I can say that if we could only put the pressure on the public authorities to use us, male or female (because, as you know, in all the advertisements today in the journal "Construction" they say, "Foreman, male or female", so there is no bar now, and you are just as young and good as you feel), a lot of money could be saved. There is much concern about the breaks and damages, the colossal sums of money which are wasted each day in these islands owing to avoidable errors by all the statutory undertakings,—G.P.O., Water Board, Electricity Board, Gas Board and all the rest, and the "cook-ups", where men are electrocuted. All this could be avoided if only they would employ members of our Society who are practical dowsers.

On farm works and on public works I have had occasion to find underground pipes, and it is no problem if you can dowse to find underground services. You can do it mentally, with your hands, or with two random bits of wire, such as I picked up on the last construction site where I was working. I broke the hazel fork and thought it would be no good walking round with that, as it would only stick through my jacket, so I picked up a length of wire and cut it in two with a pair of pliers. You can do it with fence wire or use a plumb bob on the drawings and go out and verify it on the ground. Sophisticated equipment is for the sophisticated mind. I am unsophisticated, because I am down to earth every day, no messing about, I just get on with it. If you have a problem just do what you can. If you lose your rods you go and cut off some fence wire and do it with that. You have got to resolve your problem, so you get down to basics.

In farm work it was quite interesting to pick up underground cables, underground pipes, during the redevelopment of agriculture after the war. With land reclamation there was occasion for the clearance of woodland to turn it back to agriculture. This involved the utilisation of resources such as the forest trees and also the underwood, and interestingly it included the clearance and development and utilisation of the tops of the trees. In Sussex the branches are burned for charcoal. I don't know whether you have ever seen charcoal burnt, but I have burned it and I can tell you it is quite an experience. You can either burn it in round metal bins, put the lid on, go away and forget it and come back tomorrow and it is still burning, or you can increase the value by burning it "open hearth" on a 19ft. diameter pit. In the latter case you have to live with it. It needs two of you on a 48 hour burn. You must of necessity find water, because you have to encapsulate the timber mound, which is built up in a certain way that I need not describe here. Then you have to pour water all round it and dust it and throw water round it with a bucket, like a nice big sheet and get it nice and damp on the outside. You start to light it at four o'clock in the morning and you must not leave it until it is burnt out.

Charcoal, of course, is in great demand. It is in use for moulding, for all the process moulding of the automotive industry and engineering. The moulds are automatically swashed with charcoal to prevent the metal sticking. You may perhaps realise that the deserts of the world have been created largely by man's drive for cooking materials, for charcoal and for smelting metals.

There is an old Sussex saying that if you are a dowser it puts it in a man and takes it out a woman. Well, I wouldn't like to digress on that, but in 1952 or 1953 there was a famous woman dowser (a member of this Society) in the West Country, and there was a series of photographs of her in "The Farmer's Weekly" where she was actually performing and looked as though she was being literally twisted up by the process. So there may be some truth in that saying of the old Sussex dowsers with whom I have worked. Now it has never taken it out of me, because I only do it out of necessity. If I am asked to do it, or I need to do it, I do it but I don't do it as an involuntary action.

Passing on from the activities of agriculture and forestry and coming to the major contracts in civil engineering on which I have worked, one really interesting contract on which I worked recently was at Portslade, which is farther east from here on the A27. We had an urban contract for double-tracking the A27. Now with an urban contract many of the underground services are shown on the drawings, but these drawings are not always accurate, and there is sometimes great hilarity, especially when the gas main gets broken. In the case of this contractor, who shall be nameless, they did thousands of pounds' worth of damage on a contract worth about £1.6 million. That is a lot of money to be lost. In spite of the fact that you have the water, gas, G.P.O., etc. all muddled up, all one on top of the other, it is possible to define where they are.

The contractor on the job went along the pavement area. He put the concrete down and buried all the Water Company's valve boxes. I reported to my engineers and said, "Look, if it freezes they can't shut the water off." Along came the Water Company's supervisors and they had their detectors and they started digging holes. The construction had already been put down and they marked it, but, of course, it wasn't there. They made a 4ft. hole and it wasn't there. I went along and I said, "It isn't there. It's over here." "Oh no," they said and they dug another hole in the wrong place. Eventually they weren't confounded, they were *pleased* to have my services free of charge. I went along with the superintendent and marked the position of all the services and they found them.

One interesting little story concerns a Chinese restaurant, of which we had two on the site. The Chinaman in particular watched me very closely. He didn't say much—he couldn't say much, anyway, in English. One day his restaurant filled with gas. This was caused by the disturbance of the existing construction and by the fact that the gas pipe was in a state of collapse.

Now I don't know whether you are aware of the situation in the gas industry. As we came along today they were digging up the road only two miles away. I said to my wife, "Here's another one." To put you in the picture, the reason for all these gas leaks and the unaccountable explosions is that North Sea gas is a dry gas, and in the old services the joints are screw joints with jointing compound and they won't hold North Sea gas, so the Gas Board have to come along and dig a hole up the road and a hole down the road and put a flexible nozzle right the way along the pipe and squirt a fluid in. Instead of putting a chamber at each end they seal that up; then next year they come along and dig it up again. I reckon there are more holes being dug in this country by the Gas Board than by any other industry.

However, to return to the occasion when China had gas: The general foreman said to me, "The Chinese restaurant is full of gas, John. The Gas Board are there. I think they might need you." So I went along. The foreman said, "Can you find the main?" "Oh yes," I said. "That's no problem." "Go on then," he said. "Do it for us." The contractor's interest was that the construction had already been started, so as you have to have two layers of construction road base plus black tops they had got to make a hole through that and reinstate it in the proper manner. So I found the main and they excavated and cut it off and they put a new construction in.

The Chinaman came over to me and said, "What you do with those wires?" And I said, "Not in wires, in head." "Oh yes," he said. "I tell you. When I live in Jamaica man has shop next door. You lose coat, you go to man and he say, 'Give money.' And he hold string over floor and he say, 'You no lose coat. You go back home and look in cupboard under stairs.' " I said to him, "Man Jamaica?" He said, "Oh no, man China." You may remember Major-General Scott Elliot's letter on page 188 of Journal 180, in which he suggested that "dowsing" came from the Chinese word "Taoism." That seems quite logical. The Chinese do dowse, because the restaurant keeper went on, "When I lived in China (i.e. Red China, after the war) man dig for mister make wire." "Copper ore," I said. "Yes," he said. "First time man come round hold string, go over ground, then say, 'Dig here, find water.' " He said, "No work, no water, no can drink. Then man go round hold string and say, 'Dig.' Dig down very steep. Steps all the way down." I said, "Timber?" He said, "Oh no, no timber. Very narrow. You just step down very straight. My dog he go down and for two days he no come out." It is obvious that the Chinese, even after the war, have been using this technology, as they are doing in the Soviet Union and elsewhere, to find minerals.

There was another incident when the Electricity Board found a stone slab. They called me to look at it, because as I am the Clerk of Works anything strange has to be looked at by me. I looked down the hole—it was only a small one—and saw the slab. I said, "Well, don't take it off tonight. Leave it till the morning." We lifted the slab off in the morning and I saw a chamber, which looked to me as though it was beehive shaped. They said, "It's a well," I said, "It could be but I don't think so." I went back to the drawings and found there were three pairs of houses in a line there at Portslade. So I depthed the cavities and found the width. They were 16ft. deep and 8ft. 6in. wide. I thought, "That's no well." They were cesspits! Where the gardens were being cut back they would have been underneath the new line of the pavement. If they hadn't been found, at some far distant date or some less distant date, someone would have had a great surprise. He would have disappeared in a hole down an old cesspit. My engineer said, "Don't believe it." "Well," I said, "please yourself." Then the engineer said, "We'd better give them a site order." Well, of course, they turned out to be cesspits and were filled with lime mix concrete. This shows that you can search for cavities, pipes or any object under the ground, even if it's a gas leak or a water leak.

There was another problem that arose. They had put the street lighting in in nice plastic ducts. Then along came the chaps and took up the paving stones that had all been put down and approved and they poked the compressors through the lighting ducts. That put faults into the lighting system, and this is something which the lighting people cannot easily find. They go to a lighting column and put on the impedance meter and they get a reaction which tells them that they have a break along so many feet of cable. That is all right if it is a straight line, but if it isn't they don't know where it is. I went back on the drawings and found three breaks and marked them with chalk. They dug down and there were the three breaks in the lighting system.

So you see if you can take it gradually, and if there is a demand or you can create a demand, you have a lucrative, enjoyable activity, and the public authorities must in the very near future bend towards that need.

On the present contract which I am engaged in there will be interesting archaeological finds. We have got the archaeologists out there and also there are buried statutory services. Now here is an interesting point. If you go on to an archaeological site, over a grave or tumulus you can do a count down for the number of bodies there. You can ascertain whether they are male or female, if they are children and what ages they were; you can go back in time and you can determine the date they were put in the ground. Therefore as a dowser you have the ability to go backward in time. How far forward I have not yet established!

I don't intend to continue to talk about the dowsing activities I have carried out. I would like to throw the meeting open to discussion, because I feel that is what we are here for. We are not here so that someone can spell out how good he is or what he can do because he is engaged in it daily. Really we are all here to help one another to get further understanding and appreciation of the technology in which we are involved.

DOWSING IN DORSET
H. Douglas

Two years ago I was going through Dorchester towards Bridport and noticed a car by the roadside with four people in it. I thought it was rather an unusual place to stop and wondered why on earth they were beating down all the hedges. After lunch I was asked to deal with some bees on the other side of Bridport again and noticed this car was still there. On returning half an hour later after dealing with the bees I stopped to ask if I could help. The man said " I don't think so." I replied, " But you have been here a considerable time perhaps I could." He said, " We've lost a duck." " Whatever are you doing here with a duck by the side of the main road?" I said. It appeared that this was an heirloom which had been handed down in the family for three or four generations—four and a half inches of solid brass and when you squeezed the tail the mouth opened. I asked who had handled it last and it appeared that the little boy in the back had thrown it out of the window as they had been going along. All the hedge was flat on the ground and it was far more difficult to attempt after it had been trampled down for three and a half hours. I just got hold of the child to walk up with me and I collected the duck in five minutes.

I was asked once to look at a cottage to see if it was worth buying just eight miles south of Stratford-on-Avon. During dinner some of the local legends came up as this house was reputed at one time to have been a Priory, and was still called by this name. Local people said it was haunted. However, I was quite prepared to test this so that night I slept in the attic. Nothing happened and the following morning I got up rather early and went out on to the beautiful lawn. I cast round in the garden and discovered I was on an underground tunnel. I followed this across the lawn and found it turned at right angles, went underneath a moat and right into the middle of the cottage which was for sale. This tunnel, when it was built, was a magnificent feat of engineering. It became apparent that I was on the route people took from the Priory to this cottage, which must have been the Church or Chapel about A.D. 1700. I was able to assess it from what I found in the area and judged it to be about that age. On the right of the tunnel I dowsed two yards from the house and found the skeleton of an animal which was rather large, and also of an individual. I then went to the opposite side of the tunnel again nearer the house not more than three yards from it and found a mass burial of about ten to twelve skeletons. I thought this was an extraordinary thing and the last thing I would want to do was to purchase a house like this. I went round the grounds and found in the garden thirty-eight other skeletons. When I met the owners afterwards at breakfast and told them what I had found I said that under no circumstances would I buy this property. Furthermore there should be a restraint put on any demolitions or excavations for improving the property without permission to exhume. Very few people were interested but eventually the Bristol Archaeological Society jumped at it and they found the skeleton of a horse complete with owner. They also dug out of the garden seventeen other skeletons from the mass grave which I had indicated. I saw the remains myself where they had been discovered in the underground passages. Stratford-on-Avon had a big front page write-up on it, fortunately they had not heard of me and I was the last to want publicity, but I asked them for a copy and when I returned there, of course, they wanted to take pictures and asked me to re-tell the story, but I refused. However, I returned to do a little more dowsing and this time I went back to the orchard and round the moat I found another line of seventeen, another of ten, a group of eight and on the inside of the moat eight and ten more skeletons. This was probably a mass burial from a plague at some time and obviously done in a hurry because by comparison all the others were buried very religiously. This must have been early in the history of the village perhaps before the Parish Church or many dwellings were built. It was most interesting and I should, if time had allowed, have liked to spend more time there. The water table when I was there was one foot nine inches, so you can see how difficult it was with any drainage, whether it be underground cable, water or any domestic pipes or sewers. It has now been modernised and when the builders got to the tunnel thank the Lord they did not destroy anything. They said that this building was much larger at one time basing their comments on the size of the foundations, but I think that they were wrong. The foundations they reached were the route to the tunnel and not the outside of a larger plan. It was all most fascinating.

I live in Dorset which is very rich in archaeology and there are a great many things of interest as yet undiscovered. There is still a great deal under the ground much more than the physical remains, and there are some wonderful sites like Maiden Castle and the Cerne Abbas Giant and various others which have not yet come to light. The one I am very interested in is not far from Blandford where there are lots of tumuli and mounds of earth, but I am afraid that this North Sea gas which is being installed causes desolation on many fronts and spoils barrows which are not eyesores, but which are something to cherish for all time, especially the Celtic graves. It is a crime to destroy everything above and below ground with so little consideration and only give in return the doubtful benefit of domestic gas which few of us want. It is to be hoped that they might replace and even increase the trees they destroy which would at least contribute to the future of the countryside above ground. But there will be no redress for the permanent destruction of the ancient unseen things below the soil.

At one time I was asked to investigate a peculiar mound on a private lawn. On leaving the house I found two veins of water and on going towards the mound, three steps. It is difficult to visualise just saying three steps when you can see nothing above ground, but this was so. Shortly after this the owner of the house came up with the tenant who said that they'd got a photograph of those three steps which he produced. It had been taken by the Curator of the museum, Mr. Piers, of Dorchester, and so was valuable evidence. I walked another yard and found a footing of three foot nine, further on I came on a cornerstone which when followed to the drive produced an oblong cut into three divisions. I could not decide what it was so thought that I would not make up my mind until I had surveyed the ground outside which took me about another three-quarters of an hour. In that time I found one hundred and fifty-nine graves. There were no records of these locally, Salisbury may still have something in their archives, but I doubt it. It is hard to visualise but I came to the conclusion that it was a church. The three divisions, and the steps shown in the photographs gave me the evidence I needed which was my object in dowsing for the graves. After a little further research I decided that this whole village was razed to the ground at the time of the great plague. The present parson of the new church does not know anything about this and he has not yet looked into any of the past history. One can achieve a lot by studying dowsing in archaeology which it is later possible to prove by digging. Archaeologists help in this way but I wish it were possible to work side by side with them more often, it is a pity that there are such divisions and suspicions. I for one, want to live at peace with the whole world and help everyone and that is what I do a lot of the time.

The West Country and especially Dorset is renowned for pub signs, some of which are fascinating and one in particular to me. The sign shows the picture of a headless woman, her head is underneath her arm. I have often wondered why the pub was called " The Quiet Woman " and I firmly believe that I have the answer now. A fellow came back from abroad and put in a huge acreage of apple trees, raspberries and blackcurrants after the war. This ground was pretty waterlogged and he asked me if I could help him. I found the original drains and half an hour after leaving I rang him up and said I do not think that you have told me all the facts, someone else has been here before me advising you, to which he replied, " Oh, I did not think that mattered." It turned out that he had had advice from the local drainage office and the county officials had put in the mole drains. All the original drains were going one way to a river which was correct, but the mole drains were put in straight across them with the result that the work was a complete waste of money. Although they were at the same depth they did not know and the drainage office said that there had been no drainage there before. Our fathers spent time and money making this country fertile and that's who we have to thank for the fertility of the soil. It was fertile because the drainage was done by craftsmen who knew where the springs were and who put the drains in to drain the ground at the right time and in the right amount, not ad lib as it is done now with mechanical diggers just tearing across.

To prove this point I will take you to a little site high above the village of Bexington and nearly to the top of Abbotsbury Hill.

I do not know if any of you know that area, but there is one schoolmaster in Dorset who had been using this dig for research as he wished to write a book on it when he retired. The dig had been perfectly dry until two years ago, so he asked me to investigate. I went up and found a well that was used at the time of occupation and this I thought was a mausoleum of some kind. It was perfectly well drained until a mechanical digger came in two years ago and put in new drains at a different depth from the others and sited across them. The site was now wet and water-logged and these drains had been made during the time that the school master had been working there. Anything he found had been checked by Leeds University who dated the specimens at four hundred and fifty. I found a cylindrical object far from the well which I could not understand but I felt strongly that it was worth digging. Within the cylindrical wall we found a crouch burial and later I found five others in the area. This was rather unique and we were at a loss to know why crouch burials and why the cylindrical wall? One bone was sent away to be analysed and it returned with the report that it belonged to a boy aged about twenty-five and that he had been killed as a result of his collar bone and shoulder being shattered. He must have been a hero to have been buried in that crouch position.

The mechanical digger dug one up in the field below and I found fourteen or fifteen others so it was definitely a religious burial place. But what I want to prove here is—Leeds University had dated all finds so far as 450—but when the bone came back they had altered the date to 310, which was one hundred and thirty years older than we had previously thought. It is therefore safe to assume that the drainage put down in 310 is still working! People knew what they were doing in those days, but I am afraid that there is a lot of modern drainage today, owing to subsidies, which is not so pleasing to the eye or so satisfactory agriculturally. In addition the enlarging of fields and the destruction of trees is resulting in soil erosion. If you take a visit to Cornwall where the west winds prevail, they have been sensible there and farmed with worms and humus and farmyard manure. This is the reason why the walls are there, they stop the soil blowing away, without these grassy banks built over stone to hold them firmly, there would be no humus left.

I think Cornwall is one of the most interesting and fascinating counties as regards religion and water. There were, of course, dowsers amongst the Druids so the ancient connection between religion and the finding of water held firm. Many places are marked by their Saint's prefix to show that they were religious centres, to this day they keep the names, and it is interesting to note that the ancient wells are still there. The fact that each of these places has a well and a spring is evidence that it was dowsers who provided the population with drinking water, which even today is a helpful addition to modern sources of supply.

I will move a little nearer home to give you some idea of the different jobs I am called upon to do and how disappointing it is to find that so many people do not call in a dowser until all else has failed. They try every other avenue and spend hundreds of pounds, finally they say " old so-and-so will do it " and how right they are. One particular job I handled was about five hundred feet above sea level on the side of the main Exeter road, beyond Charmouth at a place called Thistlegate. A man obtained planning permission after buying a large house which he turned into three flats to augment his income. At the same time he also got permission to turn the garage and outside buildings into houses. He had taken a lot of time and trouble in getting this permission and was just about to put the work in hand when everything was stopped by one visit of the Health Inspector. This Inspector said that the water was contaminated and that all work was to cease. Well, in came the Water Board with two or three water engineers and a mechanical digger and they started wandering round and causing havoc. At least that is what I thought privately; finally the Health Inspector for the area asked me if I would like to look into the matter. As it meant at least three day's work I said, " I am sorry but I cannot take it on." However, they pressed me so hard that I finally decided to try to help. We met the old man, the Inspector and his assistant and away we went. It required Wellingtons all right as it was a huge swamp. Incidentally, I do not use any equipment to find water; after asking for assistance and meditating for a few minutes before I start, I get down to the job, but I take good care to ask anyone who is with me on the site not to talk until I have finished.

I started to walk through this swamp, which was cup shaped and full of firs and conifers and I got five callings. I had previously told the men that when I nodded they must put a stake in the ground on the outer perimeter. This they did and when I got to the bottom I turned round and thought " Now I have got to follow the fourth one." So I walked up to this to a point where the rods went to 180 degrees in both directions and there I asked them to dig. On these jobs I always have an iron rod, shaped like a tee, and about five foot in length. With this I penetrated the ground and found what I thought was a chamber. And this is where I suggested that they dig. The owner was very indignant when I said " dig here," he added that he had had a great many men in to advise him from Exeter and from Bristol and not one of them had even made mention of the spot. However, I stuck to my guns and we dug, unearthing the container which I thought had been put in about 1840. Not a yard away

106

I got another very strong call and a little to the right there was a fifth seam calling. These two had been put in by the original owner of the property, one was for drinking and the other for driving a ram. The stench there was terrific, the pollution had obviously been caused by animals which I identified as deer. Forty or fifty deer went up there every night to drink and these fellows stayed and contaminated the water so that it was quite unfit for human consumption. I was in and out of there and managed to devise a drainage scheme in just under two hours, a job which they said would have taken them three days work. It would have been a lot cheaper for them to have a dowser in the first place rather than wasting a lot of money on people who did not know the first thing about it.

While on public health another small job and one I was quite perturbed about, involved five small children who were all living in an affected house. When I reached the place they were all ill and had been so for eighteen months. But I soon got on to the source of the trouble once they asked me to investigate. Some farmer had come to retire in this area and had bought a small bungalow a little way above the house which was being affected. He bought this in good faith and thought that everything was all right. The pump worked which was the main thing, he had got light and he had drinking water. But he had not taken sewage into consideration. The total size of the garden was eight yards by four. In that small piece of ground I found four different types of drainage plus a seam of water running downhill carrying one hundred and twenty gallons an hour. The sink and waste water ran right alongside the well and the tank where he emptied his Elsan was also nearby, yet that well was alright. But the tank leaked into a seam of water of twenty gallons an hour which went to the well in the lower garden. So that was the source of all the trouble and it was being used by the five children and their parents for drinking. You have to be very careful indeed in country areas. I continued to work in the area and told the man the depth of two wells, which when dug out were pretty accurate. Then I set about looking for some pure water and found it at what I judged to be thirty-four feet. I marked this and left it to someone who was more experienced than I to check my findings. When they finally bored they went right through four different levels so they finished up with a fine water supply.

In the town of Bridport there was a big store which kept in their cellar about two thousand pounds worth of equipment which they had the misfortune to lose overnight. They asked if I would investigate but when I referred them to the Water Board, they said that they had already been told from this quarter that their well had been overflowing. I said that this could not be but they disagreed and told the owners that it had been proved. So I decided to have a look. On calling at the office I said, " Hello, the well is here." " Yes," said the boss, " you are right on top of it." So we went down to the cellar and I had a look and the water was level with the top of the well. For eighteen months the firm had been pumping day and night on the instructions of the Council in an attempt to keep the cellar dry. But they got so tired of this and the expense it entailed that they decided to call me in. I got down and investigated in the cellar and found some silver sand. This is nothing to do with the well but it was very similar to the sand which appeared some years before in a severe frost and cracked a lot of water seams. I went out in the main road and found the main. Then I returned and found that I was not half an inch off it. Five hundred and eighty gallons an hour were leaking and had been leaking for the best part of eighteen months and all this had been going on the firm's water bill for excessive use of water. It is wrong when local authorities or these huge boards find themselves in such a position. It is they who are at fault for not having found the trouble before. The foundations of the building would eventually have gone through as a result of the sand washing out, and all the time this private firm was pumping away for them and being charged for it. This is not the first time that such a thing has happened. A few days after that I was walking up the road and I saw an inspector and I said " Hello, what's on?" He said, " We've got a leak here." I replied, " You're in the wrong place, it's down there right in the middle of the road. You dig a hole there two foot square and the pipe supply in Timothy Whites is losing two hundred and twenty gallons an hour." They opened it up and the pipe was broken off. He said, " Fancy that." Then one of the fellows working on the job said, " It's like a miracle isn't it?"

Despite the fact that they have got all the latest instruments for finding pipes, they are useless in this modern day and age when plastic and polythene pipe has taken the place of metal in the majority of water undertakings. Nothing has yet been invented to find it except a dowser, so there is lots of work for us yet. I have seen them put the earth for the electric cooker coming into the house from the mains on the plastic pipe, and they have not yet realised that when a mole wants water he does not always come to the top to drink. A mole will remove drain pipes to drink, he will eat through this if he's thirsty, God bless him. He was sent here for a purpose was the mole, he's in control of aerating the ground and yet everybody dislikes him. We all of us have our purpose which is, no doubt, the reason why we are dowsers.

WHY THE SCIENTIST DOUBTS THE DOWSER

D.M. Lewis

The " man in the street " holding uncommitted opinions must think that total lack of understanding exists between the two groups of people—scientists and dowsers. On one side we have the across-the-board statements of some scientists that dowsing has no basis in fact, while on the other side we find an unfortunate tendency for some dowsers to make seemingly unscientific statements and theories about their field.

Dowsing today is striving for recognition in a world of science and advanced technology. Scientific thought meanwhile cannot afford to ignore any aspect of natural phenomena, no matter how bizarre they might appear to be.

By some means there must be increasing dialogue between scientists and those who work in fields where it is not possible to see the application of strict laws of experimental science, as we know them today.

When invited to talk to this Society I saw it as an opportunity to do something to clarify the problem

SCIENCE versus DOWSING

Those professional scientists who are members of BSD have all been trained to look very critically for evidence before accepting any theories, or the results of experimental work. It is a good thing to be intensely sceptical in this way; all of us are prone to draw instant conclusions from vague statements and then find out that we only really know half the facts. Scientists have to look on dowsing in this critical searching manner, applying those questions that are basic and seen through all scientific work, namely, **WHY?** and **HOW?** Our critical approach must certainly be applied to our own dowsing activities. Let us say we have to be ultra-cautious about the results, and the statements we make from our experiments.

It is often very difficult for any scientist to accept some of those " theories " about dowsing that are seldom accompanied by documented experiments. We find it is not often possible to relate them to well-known and proven scientific principles unless we can examine an account of the work on which the theory has been based. It is this situation, perhaps more than anything else, that causes the scepticism expressed by the scientific world.

In my view most responsibility for dispelling this scepticism rests with dowsers. So much can be done by providing properly detailed accounts of dowsing work, and by avoiding the temptation of proposing theories, unless they can be backed by massive evidence.

For preparing my talk I have examined several years back issues of the BSD Journal to find concepts that might illustrate my points. I apologise in advance if my remarks do not agree fully with conclusions stated by some of the authors. If I am critical of some ideas and theories sincerely held by some fellow dowsers it is only to draw attention to statements most scientists will find difficult to accept.

You will be fully justified in questioning my remarks and disagreeing with statements I make. I hope this will lead to real discussion of these subjects.

" Science advances through diligent search after Truth, and the true facts can only be determined by thorough discussion of many different opinions and interpretations."

In most areas of the dowsing work we do present serious credibility problems for the enquiring scientist. It is difficult to accept that the simple tools used (or even no tools) can yield the stated results. The same tools react very differently in the hands of other operators. Why is there such conflicting advice given about techniques of dowsing? Is there no general (universally applicable) technique?

The above are simple questions. You can understand the extreme difficulty of accepting claims of map dowsing, distant diagnosis of human ailments, and so on.

There is nothing that makes dowsing more suspect to the scientific world than the almost total absence of carefully described experimental or survey work, and of results expressed in any quantitative form.

My examination of BSD Journals for the past five years located not more than one paper with *detailed* description of technique, and only one with a few quantitative results.

With these kinds of information comparison of results is quite impossible and, of course, there is no possibility of making use of statistical analysis. The results of statistical analysis of dowsing results could, I am sure, demolish much of the doubt now expressed about dowsing. Looked at in another way—when techniques are described in detail, and results given in full, preferably in numerical form, others can judge the validity of conclusions drawn about the work. Let us always remember that usually there is an alternative explanation or conclusion, and it is easy to pick on the least accurate one.

Later I will return to the subject of describing our work in such a way as to be more acceptable, not only to scientific sceptics but also among ourselves.

The general public, and not only the scientist, finds it difficult to accept the wide range claimed for dowsing activities, and also the simplicity of the tools used.

How can we explain in a convincing way that there is a way in which dowsers claim to do waterfinding—searching for missing persons—medical diagnosis—weather forecasting—food testing—

distant treatment of ailments—map dowsing and others? The usual scientific techniques of chemistry, physics, biology, can hardly claim to work in all the ways dowsing is said to do.

It is very difficult for a scientist to accept that results such as those claimed by dowsers can be obtained with such simple tools (or even no tools at all). If we consider this in a totally unbiased way it does strain one's imagination to believe that a paper clip on the end of a cotton thread, or a piece of bent wire, can tell us the location of underground streams in the Australian Outback. People naturally find it difficult to believe that some dowsers can locate missing persons by noticing the position of their twitching finger tips as they move over a map.

The scientific world today would probably look more carefully at dowsing work if the tools contained some electronics, and the results were read off from cathode ray tubes.

Acceptance of the usual dowsing tools is certainly not made easier by the different opinions on how such tools should be used.

It is interesting, but frustrating, to sort out from the Journal the many recommended methods of the various authors. The poor beginner in dowsing is made completely confused because of instructions about pendulum length, or type of Y-rod or bent wire, and whether the latter goes up or down.

In general, we now seem to agree that the tool we use is only an indicator of the dowser's reactions. Therefore I feel we should make this clear and state that a particular technique need not be the only one to give meaningful results.

Advice about samples or witnesses, as given in published articles, leads one to despair. I am not condemning their use, only pointing out that statements should not be made that samples are 100 per cent essential or effective.

The responses given by the various dowsing tools do not appear to be consistent. If a pendulum gyrates clockwise for one user what can be said if another dowser gets the opposite effect? If the effect being tested is the same there must be a great difference of response between the dowsers.

In my view we have to make clear that we have some response within ourselves and that we can be assisted by having different indicators. The scientists understand this. One will use a television screen, another a computer, and perhaps another a pen recorder, all to indicate the same effect they wish to measure.

To me the sample or witness is only an aid to concentration, it helps us to " tune " our sensitivity to what we wish to measure. It is not unusual for a scientist to pre-select ranges of measurement. Often he completely misses some important effect outside this expected range.

We now come to a tricky question which gives rise to much critical comment from the scientific world, namely, the lack of

111

precision when expressing dowsing results.

Different operators report their results in terms such as mild, very strong, weak, and so on. How does one compare the magnitudes of effects reported by different dowsers?

There is an unfortumate tendency for most people to exaggerate the extent of any stimulus they receive. It then becomes unreliable to describe any response—its magnitude depends so much on the operator's own ideas of large and small, weak and strong.

Scientists insist on actual measurements—numerical values—for all their own work, otherwise it is impossible to talk intelligibly about their results. The absence of such quantitative results from most dowsing work is a serious weakness. I do not believe there can be any real acceptance of dowsing by most scientists until means are found of expressing our results in some numerical, or graphical, form.

One cannot pick up any scientific paper, in most fields, without finding plenty of quantitative information in the form of tables of values, graphs or diagrams. In most cases scientific papers are not accepted for publication unless results are in these forms.

In contrast, however, it is extremely difficult to find papers in the BSD Journal with any numerical results. I found plenty of rather sweeping statements giving results of work, but, as a scientist, I found that no evidence was presented to justify such claims. In many cases I had to feel that the author's sweeping claims were certainly not justified by the rather vague tests he had described.

How different these papers might have been if the authors had described their work in the way long accepted for all scientific experiments:

Purpose of experiment.
Detailed account of methods.
Discussion of results.
Statement of conclusion reached.

The difficulty of experimental work. Doing experimental work in any field is difficult because of the many external factors that can interfere. Although every possible effort is made to minimise these effects, all experiments are repeated three or more times in the hope that disturbing influences will tend to cancel each other out. Even so, it is usual to do these experiments on a statistical basis, so that something can be known of the probability of any result being a chance result.

It is regarded as essential to record as many details as possible of the conditions of the experiment, and the way it was done, for other people to repeat it (and obtain confirmatory results).

Can it be said that most of the accounts of dowsing work contain enough detail to enable other dowsers to get the same results?

It is very difficult to carry out dowsing in front of an audience.

112

Some scientists therefore say that our results are not reproducible or are faked. I suggest that most scientists should be reminded of their own difficulties in demonstrating before a critical audience. It is unlikely that anyone will be found whose record of success is 100 per cent perfect. They will always attribute their failures to nervous tension.

Some dowsers talk of the hostile attitude of people in their audience causing demonstrations to go wrong. We must bear in mind, in contrast, the likelihood that the dowser is too anxious for something to happen. This is serious bias and damages any work. With a subject such as dowsing there is risk of effects being anticipated, or even imagined, so giving completely false results.

This situation can be overcome (and the result made much more convincing), by repeating any experimental work under somewhat different conditions, say, within a few hours, or on the next day, or by working in a different direction. All results must be taken into account and, in most cases, they will be found to differ significantly from each other. An average of several values will have much more validity than a single determination.

I can say from my own experience that the picture given by such repeated determinations can differ so much from a single run that one soon recognises how near it had been to making a very serious mistake.

Without repeated quantitative results such misinterpretations can occur very easily. How does one compare the significance of two results reported as " medium deflection " and " appreciable movement "? Doubtful results can easily be described if quantitative readings are not used, and nobody can be sure of what was actually done or seen.

The truth of this statement will be recognised if you examine dowsing papers in the Journal or elsewhere. People always tend to read much more into experiences than the results really warrant.

As an example of the need for fuller information about methods used, and the detailed results obtained, I can mention some very interesting work done on weather forecasting. Certain dowsing tests appeared to show a relationship between forecast results and actual weather. Unfortunately, weather is a complex subject involving sunshine, rain, wind, frost, fog, temperature and so on. What relationship did the dowsing tests show? Did they indicate days of above-average temperatures? Or periods of deep snow? Here is, unfortunately, a case where any scientist cannot accept the results. He would want to know exactly what was forecast, and would certainly want to examine the day-to-day correlation of forecast and actual conditions.

Please describe the experimental work (or survey) as fully as possible and put in the detailed results to justify the conclusions.

113

Give the reader the chance to draw the same conclusions as you have reached. But do not be surprised if he sees some other interpretation that will extend your knowledge.

The doubting scientist. With your help, persuade him to try to use the rods (these are easier for a beginner than the Y-rod or pendulum). The chances are very high that he will get a positive reaction.

The sceptic scientists cannot argue any more if he can dowse himself. On the other hand, he will feel very uncomfortable if he is one of the unresponsive minority in the population.

" There is none so blind as those that will not see." Therefore if you can show a sceptic that he himself is sensitive you have demolished his case completely.

The value of statistical methods. In talks to this Society Dr. A. R. Bailey has often referred to the use of statistics in dowsing. I agree with him completely that by applying statistical analysis we should get some really tangible evidence about the effects we find. Such results, with the supporting experimental data, could not fail to be examined carefully by the scientific world.

At the present time we do not have enough defence to the criticism that dowsing results are solely due to chance. We cannot convincingly demonstrate otherwise.

When a dowser receives reactions as shown by his rod or pendulum, which are real and which random disturbances? If he repeats his tests will he get similar results in terms of position and magnitude? Statistical methods can help to demonstrate the chances of the reactions being real ones, rather than random effects.

Statistical methods are difficult to apply unless they use numerical results of some form—the quantitative results I mentioned earlier in my talk. We must have measurements in some numerical form.

A quantitative dowsing method. Devising some dowsing techniques capable of giving numerical results may not be easy, and some BSD members may say that such methods are impossible in their field of work. Some careful thinking and ingenuity will definitely overcome this problem.

My special interests are in map dowsing, but my method can also be adapted to site work. A fuller account of the technique will appear in another paper in the Journal, so here there can be a summary of the procedure.

A pair of metal L-rods are used and graduations are marked along the long arms. As the rods deflect from their normal parallel position the crossing point occurs at some of the graduations. Strong deflection makes the readings go right up the scale. The deflection of the rods is stated as a numerical value for each point of measurement, and this value can be marked on the

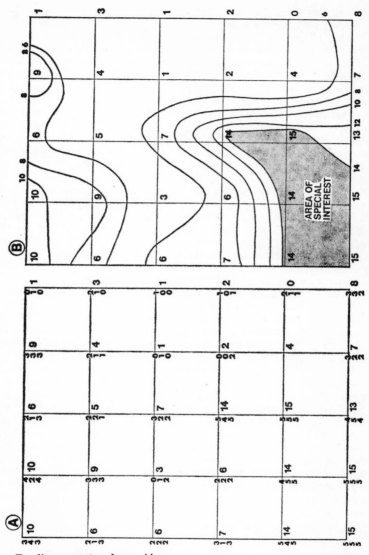

A. Readings as entered on grid.
Individual values to left of grid points.   Totals at right of grid points.

B. " Contour " map drawn from "total " points on the grid.

METHOD OF DOWSING ON A GRID LAYOUT

115

map or chart.

Doing any survey work requires strict adherence to some plan of action. In my view map dowsing is best done by following a grid laid out on the map—then the dowsing responses at each point of the grid are determined. The same procedure can be done for site work, but it can be laborious. May I say, though, that it demonstrates methodical working and cannot therefore be brushed aside as some form of trickery.

The map is worked over at least three times, the rod deflection values at each grid point being marked in. It is preferable for the grid to be traversed in different directions each time. At each point the totals of the three (or more) readings are marked in as the representative values for these particular points of the grid. These values now form the basis for drawing a contour map of the area, the contours being lines of specific reaction values.

An example of such a contour map is shown in the diagram.

What are the advantages of such a survey method, which appears to cause much more work than the dowser doing a somewhat haphazard progress over an area?

- —measurements at any one point always show much variation because of minor interfering influences. The effects of these are taken into account by the repeat traverses.
- —by totalling the values we get an impoved signal-to-noise* ratio and important features are accentuated.
- —the contour map means something to a scientist and he will examine its information. It gives him data in a form that is used in many fields.
- —the contour map with its numerical results gives us some material to which statistical analysis can be applied.

This technique appears to be capable of much refinement. Any area of the grid can be subdivided and worked over again to give results (and contour positions) in greater and greater detail.

An outstanding advantage of such a method is the way it can prevent rather wild statements being made about some dowsing results. It prevents sweeping generalisations such as the North Sea oil and gas fields, for instance, being shown as hundreds or thousands of square miles in extent, when, in fact, they are small and localised, usually only some tens of square miles in area.

Conclusion. While critical of various aspects of dowsing as it exists today, it is hoped that my comments will provoke some careful thought. I tried to make all criticism constructive.

The energy crisis in which we exist today makes it essential to find new sources of coal, gas and oil. New supplies of water are essential to satisfy our needs. Today there are unrivalled opportunities to show what can be achieved by dowsing, and within BSD there is a strong wish to demonstrate what can be done. But the work we do must, in some way, become more acceptable to the Government, public bodies, the oil companies and others.

People will be more ready to listen when results are presented in a more scientific form and without all-embracing statements based on *inadequate facts*. Let us provide more information about our actual dowsing work and make our results more credible to those who genuinely find it difficult to accept what we say we can do.

Let us bother less about elaborate theories of dowsing, keeping such discussions out of our practical work. Such theories and deep arguments about the relationship of dowsing with religion, the supernatural and so on, should be the field of work of philosophers in our Society.

Nothing damages our standing more, in the eyes of scientists, than the tendency to mix up practical dowsing with obscure philosophical ideas.

---

* For the benefit of readers to whom the expression " signal/noise ratio " is unfamiliar, Mr. Lewis has written the following explanation:—

A dowser walking along any path (or indeed doing any kind of search) should find the rod, or other indicator, is constantly alive in his hands. It gives no obvious response, as when deflected by some *signal*, yet the rod seems to be shivering or making slight but irregular movements. This has to be expected, because there should be some slight response to materials in the ground, or underground water, for example. This irregular response can be regarded as *noise*. It is essential that the *signal* should be far stronger in its effect than the *noise* level. In other words, the dowser must strive for a very high signal/noise ratio.

As an example of getting a poor signal/noise ratio one can consider a dowser looking for underground water in a marshy field. The immediate sub-surface water should be causing continuous response of the dowsing tool, yet the dowser must try to detect the much stronger signal that is important for him.

In some fields of work, especially searches for minerals (or oil or gas) the desired material is dispersed over a considerable area, although the amount varies from place to place. It is of no value for the dowser to say the material is there—he must be fairly specific about the amounts (that is, how the ore is distributed). The dowser's results must then be expressed in some quantitative form, that is, he must measure his responses. The irregular responses (the background noise) can then be a serious nuisance, because it obscures the real *signal*. Some method must be used to improve the signal/noise ratio.

In the technique mentioned in my lecture, three or more surveys are made over the same area. The *noise* values are likely to differ from one survey to another, but the true signals should have about the same value each time. Therefore by adding the results for each survey the differences between signals and noise become more obvious. The example below will make things clearer.

VALUES

Survey A	3	2	2	0	7	2	3	1
Survey B	2	1	1	1	6	3	4	2
Survey C	2	2	1	0	7	3	4	0
Totals:	7	5	4	1	†20	8	†11	3

The significance of the signals (†) becomes clear.

Some dowsers will probably object to my comments above, claiming that they never experience any " noise," but that all signals are 100 per cent sharp. This is contrary to normal human experience, where actual facts must always be sorted out from a mass of confusing and irrelevant information.